Jojo

Jojo

Finally Home

Johannes Radebe

First published in Great Britain in 2023 by Hodder Catalyst
An imprint of Hodder & Stoughton
An Hachette UK company

5

Copyright © Johannes Radebe 2023

This Work was written by Paul Modjadji in conjuction with the Author. This Work was edited by Georgina Rodgers.

A CIP catalogue record for this title is available from the British Library

Hardback ISBN 9781399722711
Trade Paperback ISBN 9781399722728
ebook ISBN 9781399722735

Typeset in Electra by Hewer Text UK Ltd
Printed and bound in Great Britain by Clays Ltd, Elcograf S.p.A.

Hodder & Stoughton policy is to use papers that are natural, renewable and recyclable products and made from wood grown in sustainable forests. The logging and manufacturing processes are expected to conform to the environmental regulations of the country of origin.

Hodder Catalyst
Hodder & Stoughton Ltd
Carmelite House
50 Victoria Embankment
London EC4Y 0DZ

www.hoddercatalyst.co.uk

Contents

To my Mama.

Preface

Here We Go . . .

Dear reader,
Darling, out of the millions of books you could have read right now, thank you so much for choosing mine. Growing up, I aspired to be part of something that represented me and told my story. I found expression through dance; the rhythms and beats that touch your soul, and the sparkle of sequinned, tactile costumes . . . The fact that I now do this so publicly, through *Strictly Come Dancing* and my two headline tours, *Freedom* and *Freedom Unleashed*, feels like a beautiful blessing for which I will be forever grateful.

Now, I get to tell my story in my own words. From growing up in Zamdela, a township in South Africa, to unexpectedly stumbling across dance classes and becoming a two-time Professional South African Championships winner and three-time Amateur Latin South African Champion, to prime-time TV with a stint working on cruise ships in between, I have always just wanted to work and do what I love: to make myself and the people around me proud. But I knew I was different, even as a flamboyant child who loved to twirl in the street and, often, I just wanted to blend into the background. As a six-foot-plus gay boy with a penchant for feathers and heels, you will understand that this was not always that easy, and I have suffered my fair share of trauma and adversity along the way.

As I write, it is New Year's Eve 2022, and I am home for the Christmas holidays. I'm sitting in my bedroom in my mum's home in Zamdela, with the door shut and the lights off. The family has gathered to celebrate the dawning of a new year. Through the pitch dark, I can smell the rich, languid tang of the barbecue – or braai, as we South Africans call it. It is a happy day here at the Radebe home; the low thrumming sound of music, the chattering buzz of conversation and sweet children's laughter fill my mum's dusty yard. Unlike British winters, the air is warm and balmy, with a soft breeze from the window. I am back in the warm embrace of my family. I am so thankful.

The past year of my life has been a whirlwind of emotional extremes. I have endured the deepest, gut-wrenching pain I've known against the backdrop of the most euphoric highs. I have witnessed the lowest pits of grief with the passing of my Aunt Martha, which led me to seek therapy and help deal with the complexity of trying to understand myself and my feelings. My life was then forever altered by *that* season of *Strictly Come Dancing*. John Whaite and I made history together as the first same-sex male couple on the show – a moment dubbed a 'culture shift'; we upended the narrative. Although I was unravelling emotionally at that moment, the public response to it was overwhelmingly positive. Much to our astonishment, John and I would progress to the final, thanks to the fans who voted for us week after week. The people had spoken unanimously. We were publicly accepted as an unorthodox couple on a vast public platform, and that was something to behold. It was a monumental first; not just for us, but for so many others out there watching.

Back at my mum's, I'm struck that I'm reunited with friends and family, but a feeling of discord meets the initial happiness of hugging them and being skin-to-skin again; my heart feels like it's been chipped. I only want to sit quietly and sink deeper into whatever is happening inside. Throughout my life, an army of women has raised and nurtured me; they have always been in front of and backstage in my life. The invisible thread that runs between me and them – my mum, Granny Jane, Aunt Martha, Aunt Patricia – is unbreakable. I have not made peace with the passing of my Aunt Martha. Due to Covid-19 restrictions on travel at the time, I couldn't travel from London to South Africa for her funeral. On the day, I heaved myself out of bed and dressed in my smartest black suit and shiny shoes. I knew she would expect that of me. I watched the ceremony on a screen, blurred through tears. I could feel the pain of my family thousands of miles away. Their howls reverberated, swelling through me. I longed to hold them and for them to hold me.

During this visit home, on Boxing Day, I went to her grave. I stood beside that patch of land and sobbed like a child. All I could think of was that people like my aunt don't belong in the ground. She was the picture of health and vitality. A strong, pioneering woman, she fearlessly owned every room she walked into and lived as though she would be around forever, with a sense of measured but unapologetic ownership. She was my hero and someone on whose character I'd tried to shape my own. It feels like my aunt's final lesson to me. Her ultimate message: to live fully. To always own the moment. To never fear or pull back out of fear. My family's clan name is 'Mthimkhulu'. It implies a pioneering spirit; nothing is insurmountable for us. I know I will make it through this.

Writing this book has been one of the most cathartic and healing experiences of my life. Our days are made up of thousands of tiny moments, experiences and lessons. In *Finally Home*, I reveal personal moments that have shaped me into the man I am in this world. I intend to share parts of my story which I have kept buried away – the poignant, as well as the cheerful and thrilling moments that have propelled, coloured and peppered my life with splendour, joy and goodwill; the moments that have paved the way for new beginnings.

This book is for anyone who wants to be seen. I'm no activist, but my mum – who grew up during the Apartheid years – recently said to me: 'Our generation had a purpose. We were fighting for your freedom, and now you have it; what are you going to do with it?' I want to show you a different narrative. I have always said you can't be what you can't see. Whatever your differences – and after all, isn't that what makes life so interesting, so full of magic, sparkle and joy? – know that I understand you; I see you and hear you.

I will continue speaking out for everyone to feel free, to have their rights and to be heard and understood.

Love from Jojo xxx

Chapter One

Flying the Nest

As a child, one of my favourite pastimes was playing with my older sister, Jabulile, and her impressive collection of dolls. She had a hoard of plastic Barbies, and we would sit together for hours in the dirt yard, plaiting their long hair and making up stories about their escapades. I adored their tiny outfits – miniature dresses, shirts and shorts – sliding them over their feet and securing them behind their long necks, setting them up in their best clothes for whatever we had in store for them. Once the clothes were on, our play would stretch for hours as the sun dropped on the horizon, like time was almost elastic, the air still thick with the warmth of the day.

There was a dump site not far from our home called Belina and, even though my mum hated me going there because it was dangerous, sometimes I would slip away and see what treasures I could find. People would dump all kinds of things there, from old furniture to books and toys. I was always looking for a glimpse of abandoned clothes and, some days, I landed on bright strips of material that I would hastily collect and bring home, my hands held high as if clutching a prize. My mum taught me to thread a needle and create a tiny outfit with all the stitching hidden on the inside. Sitting together, we would sew tiny stitches, so they looked amazing.

In those early years, Dad was an amazing provider. He was a merchandiser for Coca-Cola and brought back footballs and basketballs. I had so many; I gave them to my friends and neighbours. I knew he wanted me to love ball sports because he was a football star, known as 'Fly' by his friends because none of them could keep up with him on the field. But he could see that ball sports didn't hold my interest and after a while, he gave up. One day, when I was about six, he came home with vouchers instead.

'Go and buy yourself whatever you want,' he told me and my sister.

We walked to a shop in town, which was called OK. It sold food, hardware, toys and must-have stuff – a bit like Tesco. My sister rushed to the chocolate aisle and I raced off to find something that took my fancy.

As I emerged with a box, Jabulile looked at me and what I was carrying.

'Is that what you are going to buy?' she asked, smirking.

It was a knock-off Barbie – a plastic doll with long hair and a beautiful figure, with a pinched-in waist and elegant neck, prime for a new outfit. I wanted to finally have my own doll because I was tired of my playtime being at the mercy of my sister's moods. Some days she was happy for me to share, while on others, she locked the dolls away, out my reach.

I felt slightly nervous about my dad's reaction when I arrived home. Deep down, I knew he would rather I brought home a replica gun, another ball to add to the collection or a plastic car.

So I reasoned that I would tell him it was my latest mannequin for making clothes.

'I bought chocolate, but your son bought a Barbie doll,' Jabulile announced. Seven years older than me, she was a teenager and getting a bit of a mouth on her.

The room was silent. No one challenged me, and everyone's expressions were neutral.

'Phew, that was easy,' I thought, and off I went into my room to find a needle, thread and some material.

At home, I was raised very much isolated and protected, in the warm cocoon and love of my family. Mum didn't like me playing in the streets. Many other children would spend their days outside together, kicking balls in the dust and making innocent mischief. In those days, entertainment like television and children's books were not bountiful, especially in places like Zamdela, Sasolburg – a mining township in what was then the Orange Free State in South Africa. Zamdela had developed under the Apartheid Group Areas Act of 1950, which pushed people of colour to the margins of major cities and grouped them according to cultural and racial background.

My father, Pule Benjamin Radebe, my mum Jocobeth, Jabulile and I lived in a modest four-room breeze-block bungalow with my paternal grandma, Jane. Our home, like the others around us, was modest. My parents shared a bedroom, and I shared a room with my granny and sister. We lived on top of each other and loved each other fiercely. My early childhood was one of the happiest times of my life because it was the one time my family was together – a unit that was so cohesive that everything just fell into a natural and happy rhythm. I was born into a situation where we had everything and wanted for nothing. We weren't rich by a long stretch. Yet, we had each other, and you cannot put rand on that. There was always food on the table, clothes on our backs and a lot of laughter and love, which I attribute mainly to the efforts of my grandma, who was at the centre of everything, and my mum.

My father was Jane and Johannes Macala Radebe's only child. Sadly, Grandpa Johannes, after whom I am named, passed away before I was born. Granny Jane was a staunch Christian. By the time I was born, she was already elderly. Petite with a slight hunch, she was softly spoken and still quite energetic. We called her 'Mme', a Sesotho word that means 'mother', pronounced 'mm-eh'. Mme was one of the most complex and fascinating women I have ever known. As old as she was, she could not be held down. Not even her hunchback could stop her from cleaning, cooking and running the household like a slick business operation, bustling around like a mouse instead of the turtle she sometimes resembled. My mum would also work hard to keep our house in order. She was the perfect wife and mother in that respect and took great care looking after the home and us, waking in the early hours of the morning to sweep our yard with a lefielo, a handcrafted twig and grass broom.

When I woke up, there would always be incredible smells emanating from the kitchen as Mme cooked breakfast. Breakfast was porridge made with maize meal and milk, which has a creamy and firm texture. Sometimes my parents and Granny ate it with vinegar and sugar. I preferred mine with the sheen of newly melted butter floating atop. We always ate food you could grow in the ground, like marrows, beetroot, broad beans, potatoes, cabbage and carrots. There was also a local market that Mme used to swear by because it sold the freshest veggies. She would buy whatever was there – say, pumpkin – and cook it in many different ways. We would have pumpkin stew, mashed pumpkin with melted butter and pumpkin pie. It was never the same dish twice and, as a child, it was always so exciting to find out what Mme and Mum would conjure up in our tiny kitchen space.

I was always with my mum and, while she never allowed me to touch anything, I would watch her busy around the kitchen cooking, and I learned a lot about the best ways to cook certain foods. On Sundays after church, we would cook all the vegetables at the same time; this was known as 'seven colours'. Pudding was always our treat of the week – canned peaches with home-made custard and jelly. I revelled in that dish. Meals with meat were rare and a delicacy. We enjoyed tripe, and sometimes there were ritual slaughters of chickens, sheep, cows or goats to show gratitude to God, asking for protection or healing from our ancestors. This is a South African tradition that dates back hundreds of years.

One of my favourite childhood memories is sitting under the grapevine in our front yard. Every year, without exception, it would bear the biggest, sweetest green grapes imaginable. My mother, Mme and I would spend countless afternoons under it, laughing and feasting on the fruit until the juice dripped over our hands and chins. I knew my favourite time of the year – the summer months – had arrived whenever I caught sight of those first green gems.

With my dad at work and sister at school, when I was very small I was always in the company of other adults and sat in the shadow of my mum and Mme. I was never out of my mum's sight. We didn't have a TV, but my mum and Mme would listen to dramas on the radio. When I tried to speak to them, they would always hush me. 'Quiet, Baba,' they would say. (I was named after my grandfather and 'Baba' means father so this was the name I was given as a sign of respect to him and the role he played within our family. I was expected to follow in his footsteps.) So I would sit quietly playing, mostly lost in my head, a make-believe world of stories and adventures.

Then, in the late afternoon, their friends would come and sit. Some worked as cleaners in neighbouring white suburbs, and this was a time to unwind, play cards or gossip about developments in the township. We later discovered that the tea parties Mme and her ladies would host were not always just tea parties. It turned out they were quaffing beer from their pristine China teacups. For years, we were none the wiser until, one day, Jabulile unceremoniously exposed my grandmother. Mme was many things – a God-fearing woman, wife, mother, grandmother, and community and church leader. But she didn't like it to be known that she drank alcohol. She was mortified that Jabu had caught on to her secret. I could see it in the flush of her cheeks, but we all howled with laughter.

*　　*　　*

My father was an ordinary lad, doing everyday things that men did in Zamdela. He came home every evening and provided for his wife and family. There was warmth and safety in our home. Football – or soccer as we call it – was a big deal for us too. Dad was a die-hard Kaizer Chiefs supporter, while my mum supported the Orlando Pirates. Many nights, the two would not speak to each other because the Pirates had beaten Dad's beloved Chiefs. Then there were evenings when my father would keep us up until the early hours, blasting his victory music.

A timeworn tradition, my father would socialise with other men at the local bar after work and, at the weekend, he would go to a nearby stadium to watch football. He would often take me to watch key fixtures, and I treasured spending time with him and his friends. I was usually the only youngster among the grown men and would be showered with snacks and sweets. It was the one time that I could get almost anything I wanted from my father. Those weekends at the stadium were golden to me. Besides the sugar rush, this was our exclusive father-and-son time. It was our thing, and I looked forward to it. The ritual of getting ready, catching a minibus taxi and spending the day together was unrivalled. Sometimes, if the weather unexpectedly changed and there was a downpour, my father and I would go and buy matching outfits so that we could change out of our sodden clothes.

We lived cheek by jowl with our neighbours. Living in the UK now, the silence shocks me so much sometimes. In Zamdela, you can hear your next-door neighbours sneeze and their every utterance. There was no hiding, and we all knew each other back to front. While there were arguments and difficult circumstances, my overriding memory was the fact that everyone shared what they had. No one ever complained of hunger. If someone did not have enough food, they could go next door and get a piece of bread. We welcomed people into our home. If someone in the community needed something, we would all show up to help; everyone looked out for their neighbours. There was also a palpable energy with so many people and personalities in one place. As soon as the sun rose in the morning, soaring high into the sky and scorching the mud and dirt beneath, the place would come alive with the noise of chickens clucking, music playing and people laughing, talking and shouting. It was electric. The volume turned down only when the sun set – sometimes just to dial back up again if there was a party. There is a unique intensity to living like that. I was loved so intensely that I never saw myself as different to other boys or less than anyone else. The heat of the sun and my family's love enveloped me like a warm blanket.

My grandmother introduced me to God and a spiritual path of prayer and faith. On Sundays throughout my childhood, Mme would ensure I was bathed, my skin smeared with Vaseline and my hair neatly brushed before adorning me in my finest threads. Then, off we would go to church where Mme was an elder, a position that bestowed her with the honour of wearing the immaculate black-and-white uniform reserved for community seniors. As soon as I could walk, I was dressed from head to toe in a matching outfit – a crisp white shirt and black trousers – that would be tailored by my mum to fit. I was a young child dressed like a forty-five-year-old, but, as a family, we cared about looking smart and making great efforts to look our best.

Dad was a Lepantsula. Lepantsula is an expression of cultural roots and more than about fashion and music, but a way of life in the townships. His clothes were pressed and polished – plaid trousers with creases down the front, stylish wool sweaters from brands like Pringle and a newsboy cap; it was a universal look borrowed from classic American and English styles, and a declaration of self-worth and care in the days of Apartheid. The way he wore his clothes was a cut above.

I loved Sundays because we would all hop into a minibus and drive forty-five minutes to church in Sebokeng. My family would parade me around, and my hair would be ruffled and my cheeks squeezed. Even though I grew tall later on, as a boy I was small and comfortable talking to anyone. Everyone was so lovely to me. As I drove to church each week, hot in my suit, we passed white suburbs, where manicured lawns, bright-blue private swimming pools and white-washed villas with barbed-wire high walls would whizz by through smeared windows, but I didn't think anything of this. They had what they had, and we had what we had. That's where my thoughts about the differences ended back then.

I was born on 27 April 1987, during one of South Africa's most politically turbulent years. Less than three years after I was born, Nelson Mandela was released from Robben Island, having served twenty-seven years in prison for his anti-Apartheid activism, advocating for equality and justice. Apartheid was a system of institutionalised racial discrimination and segregation that was enforced by the South African government from 1948 until May 1994, when Mandela became South Africa's first democratically elected president.

Apartheid aimed to maintain white minority rule and denied basic rights and opportunities to the Black population. Mandela played a role in undoing this and led negotiations with the South African government, working towards reconciliation, leading to the dismantling of Apartheid laws. All I knew was that Mandela was a hero and would save us all. In the townships, we celebrated his rise to power like the best birthday party of our lives; everyone went into the streets and, everywhere I looked, people were cheering.

The beginning of a new journey for my country was also the backdrop to my formative years. Growing up, I had the sense of being 'born free', the name used for South African people of colour after the end of Apartheid. In the township, life was modest, but there were boxing clubs, recreation centres and football clubs. We were constantly reminded that we had opportunities and, importantly, these chances had not been afforded to the older generation. As I grew up, doing nothing was not an option. Our freedoms had been hard-won. There was generational trauma in our wake and, as I have grown older, that realisation and understanding has become even more evident to me. But back then, the overriding sense from the generation before us was that we needed to be the change and live a full – and free – life.

As South Africa battled to chart a new path and map out a fresh future, I was beginning primary school. Tsatsi Primary was just a few minutes' walk from my home. In the build-up to starting school, my mum helped ensure my uniform was the perfect fit. I was skinny, so she took in my shorts.

'Mama, I'm scared,' I told her as she nimbly pinned my clothing, her needle and thread working deftly through the seams.

'Baba, don't you worry. There are people who will look after you. If anything happens, I am here.'

For the first time, I would leave the comfort and safety of my mum and Mme, and face the world on my own, surrounded by other little people for hours on end. I was comforted by the fact that the school gates would be open at all times. There was never enough food to go around from the food scheme, where local businesses gave bread with peanut butter and milk. This was always saved for kids who lived a long way away, so the teachers would encourage those of us who lived nearby to leave at lunchtime and go home to eat before coming back for afternoon lessons.

I found school both exciting and terrifying; every bubble of exhilaration about the novelty of being away from home and the familiarity of my family was very quickly met with a flash of fear. Everything was new and unfamiliar. The only security I had was Jabulile, who went to the same school and could walk with me there. Once we arrived, though, I was left to navigate it on my own. Many species of birds throw their young from the nest to force them to learn to fly. Going to school was me unceremoniously leaving the nest.

I made new friends, mostly with soft and kind girls who took me under their wing. Very quickly, it felt like a magical place to be. Ms Buang, one of my teachers, was a larger-than-life character. She was short and stout, with a kind, round face and a heart as big as the classroom. She wore bright, colourful outfits and sang to us, creating beautiful rhymes and singalongs that helped us grasp the lessons and concepts she was trying to teach. She was our teacher, and we were her babies. There was no other teacher like her.

Between Ms Buang, the other teachers and hanging out with my new friends, it was magnificent – for a while, particularly in those first few weeks when the new arrivals familiarised themselves with the surroundings and each other. Over forty of us would sit crammed like sardines into the stuffy classroom, two to a desk. For the first time, I was learning new things: maths, reading, writing and colouring in. I loved waking up and getting dressed in crisp, freshly ironed khaki shorts, matching short-sleeved shirts, long black socks and shiny black shoes.

In those days, township schools operated with strict rules. Children were expected to be on time and dressed neatly in uniform. No backchat of any kind was permitted. Teachers were in authority, and they were not to be questioned. Schoolwork had to be done. Corporal punishment was still a thing back then. Bad behaviour was called out, and kids were given a beating on the hands or bottom with a hard stick covered in Sellotape. As parents dropped their kids off at school, teachers were given verbal permission to use that stick on those who stepped out of line.

'Yes, he must do his work. If not, give him a hiding.'

If our mums were called, we would be getting a hiding at home as well as at school, so there was no escaping it. It was just how life was, and we never questioned that. I was determined to be the school's best goody-two-shoes.

I remember this part of my life with sharply divided emotions. I learned how cruel and unkind children can be. Even though I had made some friends, I was picked on and marked out as different from the beginning. I was a bit too flamboyant but desperately wanted to be happy to be like the other boys. I was a 'sissy boy'. At first, I wasn't much bothered by it. It was just words, and I accepted that I was a different kind of child. Long before school, I knew I was not like the other boys in my family and around me.

Initially, I didn't fully understand what the word 'sissy' meant. I instinctively knew it was derogatory and related to my feminine nature. By contrast, I knew I was loved, protected and doted on at home. Perhaps Mum knew better when she kept me safe at home, away from the streets. I had to grow a thicker skin.

There was a day when our teacher told us to bring things in from home, like toys and games; it would be a day of fun and not lessons.

'Are you sure we can bring anything?' I asked Ms Buang.

'Yes, there is no schoolwork. So, bring your favourite things,' she replied. 'Bring whatever you like, Johannes.'

Together with my little group of friends, we decided to bring our dollies. As you can imagine, my dollies were dressed to kill.

By the end of the first term at school, I already knew that, as a boy who played with Barbie dolls at home, this would not be a place I could be fully myself. As a township with mining and industrial origins, many of its people were from rural parts of the country. Many of them had conservative, even old-fashioned, and traditional views. The idea of a boy who appeared feminine and flamboyant like me sent them off the deep end. They goaded me about how I spoke, walked and carried myself:

'Are you a girl, sissy boy?'

'You walk funny . . .'

'Why do you talk like a girl?'

As much as I resented these crude observations being thrown in my face, I took it in my stride. Most children want to belong, blend in and make friends. At that age, the idea of being an individual and embracing your uniqueness is often not developed – or encouraged; you want an easy life. I kept telling myself that if I continued to turn up at school unfazed and strong, they would eventually get over it and learn to love and accept me.

But, to my horror, this was not easy, and quickly the bullying spread to boys outside my immediate classroom. The only places I could ever feel safe were at home or in the classroom, and walking outside became an ordeal. After the school bell had rung, I was fair game for predators. This was understood by the students, teachers and parents alike; it went unspoken in the glances between teachers and other knowing adults. I soon discovered I was also at risk of attack from ignorant adults who behaved like kids and chided me.

On the days when my sister had to stay behind for supplementary classes or extracurricular activities, I would be targeted and tormented on my way home. It got so bad that some boys would chase me, throwing punches, and I would run as fast as I could, feeling my heart pounding out of my chest and dust flying in my wake. My sister would continuously have to fight off bullies on my behalf.

'Leave him alone,' she would shout at them, right in their faces.

As absurd as it sounds, I learned to accept this as part of my journey. Unfortunately, I didn't have an option. At that point, the idea that I could alter myself had not entered my mind, but I did start to dread going to school. In the morning, I would feel my stomach churn with nerves, and the palms of my hands would become clammy as I was doing up my shoelaces. The excellent teachers who ensured I was safe in the classroom and my handful of friends made going to school bearable and kept me going.

Many times, I would return home in tears, the collar of my shirt sodden with the trials of the day. At first, I was reluctant to tell my mum what was happening. I didn't want to get in trouble or make a fuss. One time, though, she drew it out of me.

'Why are you crying, Baba?' she yelled. She was angry; I could feel the flames of rage coming off her.

'Baba, today you're going tell me what happened,' she said, sitting me down and staring so hard into my eyes I knew I needed to tell her the truth. I had never seen her so incensed. In my confused state, I didn't know precisely where her anger was directed.

With tears pouring down my face, I told her that I had been harassed and physically attacked by a group of boys who were calling me names. My mum took a deep breath, wiped the tears off my face and brought me a glass of water.

After letting us both cool down, she calmly said: 'Baba, you are who you are. I love you, and that should be enough.'

We talked about it and how I would handle it.

'I want you to know that, whatever happens to you, you can tell me. I love you and will always love you.'

She chose to bring us closer during a moment which she could have chosen to make about those bullies. At that age, I couldn't comprehend the gravity of what my mother was communicating to me. I just knew the feeling I was left with. I felt loved and valued. Mum didn't set out to avenge me or to stop the bullies. Instead, she asserted her love as something bigger than what those kids had said. Without using any label, Mum found a way to tell me she accepted and loved me. That was the most powerful and liberating message this little gay boy, who played with Barbie dolls, occasionally wore his mum's heels and was bullied at school, could ever hope to hear. I have held on to the memory of that day ever since. It has often remained with me when I doubted my worth or place in this world. It also cemented the bond of trust between me and my mum – trust that still exists and gets stronger with every passing day. I can share anything and everything with her.

Chapter Two

Stumbling Into Dance

In the mid-nineties, South Africa, just like the United States, had a musical reawakening. As the world witnessed the renaissance of American nineties hip-hop and R&B, South Africa bore its own music genre called kwaito – the freedom sound. Kwaito is characterised by upbeat sounds reflecting life in the country's townships and capturing the exuberance and excitement of liberation. It draws on electronic, dance, pop and hip-hop music to create a combination of house beats and vocals sung in South African colloquial languages. Kwaito was such a visceral and affecting sound, and it had the entire country spellbound.

One of the bands that struck me and my friends the most was a quartet called Boom Shaka. Boom Shaka set the country ablaze with its talent and dance moves. During performances, the legendary Lebo Mathosa and her bandmate, Thembi Seete, would gyrate, kick and twerk their bodies in a way the country had never before seen. The girls' dance moves were an expression of who they were, and they weren't afraid to show it.

When I was about six, around the time I started school, my dad bought a TV home. It was met with wild excitement – after so many years of radio, having picture and colour was a beautiful thing. It gave us something to do as a family, and we never missed any programmes. From about half past six in the evening, we would gather around to watch whatever was on. We would sit together in the dining room and eat our dinner while we watched. The first time I saw Boom Shaka, I wasn't sure how I processed it; my only thoughts were that they looked incredible and moved their bodies in a way that left my jaw open.

'Oh my God,' Mum said, equally shocked for a different reason. 'They are wearing next to nothing.'

My parents were conservative, and Boom Shaka's fashion and music embodied changing times and our collective response to newly won freedoms. Everyone lost their minds when the sounds of Boom Shaka's 'It's About Time' – their most popular hit at the time – roared from speakers in minibus taxis or people's yards. In townships all over South Africa, people put loudspeakers outside their homes and played music as loudly as they could as soon as the weekend arrived.

Boom Shaka would tour the townships. In Zamdela, a man called Ntate Tshehla would trundle up and down the streets of the township with a loudspeaker, announcing the news every day. He would call out details of upcoming community meetings, funerals of much-revered members of the community, political rallies – you name it – and the news would criss-cross the township to reach the ears of the right people. When he announced that Boom Shaka was about to pitch up in Zamdela, I ran as if my very existence hinged on it, with my two friends, Jeffrey Thulo and Seun Mpetjekane, to get near the front of the crowd. Big brands would sponsor the performance, so they arrived in a large truck advertising detergent. Out they came, all flesh and sound. We were not near the front, having been out-run by bigger kids and teenagers, but I can remember the roar of the crowd. It was deafening. The technology was crude, but the crowd sang along in one loud voice. Boom Shaka was larger than life. Even as a young child, I felt liberated. My friends and I looked at each other; we wanted to be just like them.

One of my biggest breakthroughs at school came when I made friends with Jeff and Seun. Jeff and I were in the same year, and Seun was two years above us. Seun was friends with my neigh-bour, Mona, who was also queer like me and moved and spoke differently. Mona looked out for me. When Mona introduced us, I immediately felt we had the same energy and moved in a similar effeminate and flamboyant way.

'Oh, my goodness, *who* are they?' I thought silently before saying a cool 'hi'.

When Jeff announced one day that he had a 'boyfriend', we gathered around and discussed the details. They accepted me for who I was. In contrast, my cousins were quite masculine, and that was highlighted when I was in their company; I was just different from them – a bit more animated, more delicate and I carried myself differently. I was always called 'special' by them. I knew I was not the same, but it never felt like anything was wrong with that in our home. There were often mumblings between adults about this that I overheard, but it was never a problem – more of an observation.

When I was at school, it was a different matter. Jeff, Seun and I were fighting a common threat. Like me, Seun and Jeff were also called 'sissy boys'. Together the three of us would help each other navigate those early years of being targeted and bullied. It brought such shame. We became each other's fortress. Together with other classmates, we escorted each other home and were a force to be reckoned with, and we had made a pact to look out for each other. The comfort I found in them was greater than any other friendship.

I always wanted to run away from trouble, but Jeff and Seun had no such qualms. What I lacked in confidence, they made up for in spades.

'Yeah, I'm a sissy boy. AND?' They would say, spinning around to face the perpetrators. They would take them on.

'Please. If you respond like that, they are going to come for us,' I would say to them, nervous about what any altercation could lead to.

'Well, they come, and we show them,' Jeff and Seun would reply, unfazed.

Of course, nothing ever happened because they had clawed back the power. I knew their presence tipped the balance of control, so I hung on to them like a pest.

It was by pure chance that I would discover my life's passion. One ordinary Saturday, when I was seven, I left home to look for my friends. My mum, always protective, did not love me doing this, but, when I had nothing to do, I would head out to find someone to spend time with. Then, if my friends and I felt particularly brave, we would sometimes head to the public swimming pool, which was quite some distance away. I always tried to hide that we had been that far from my mum, but it was never easy with red eyes stinging from chlorine and wet underwear.

For some reason, Jeff, Seun and my other friends were nowhere to be seen that Saturday, so I decided to look for my sister instead. Sometimes, I would try to hang out with my sister and her friends; they were easy company and we had some of the same interests, like playing skipping rope and home-made board games. But, on this day, my search for her yielded no results either. The streets were ominously empty, with only the odd farmer guiding cows or donkeys through the streets to graze nearby. It looked like the township had been deserted. My next-door neighbour told me that my sister was at the recreation hall. This was a modern building where meetings and indoor sports like volleyball took place. People would also use the space for church ceremonies and weddings.

Off I went to look for her. Everyone was engrossed in learning modern dance as I stepped through the doors, including my sister and her friends. The girls were genuinely having fun. The boys seemed to be there for the girls, looking at them with wide eyes. Everyone was mesmerised.

'Come in, come in,' said one of the trainers, beckoning me inside. I joined the crowd, looking for my friends.

A new dance club was being launched and the founders, Abuti Ben Mosia and Ausi Mpho Kheswa, were giving demon-strations to persuade us children to join. During the mid-nineties, community talent competitions inspired by the American and kwaito contemporary dance groups of the era were popular. Friends would join together to compete, typically for the title of the best group. Through the Boiketlong Vital Dance Club, Abuti Ben and Ausi Mpho intended to assemble all these groups and develop them into one solid force that could compete nationally and represent Zamdela. It was a novel idea for our small township.

Abuti Ben and Ausi Mpho taught us a short modern dance routine that day. I remember the delight on all our faces as we memorised the moves. Through my young eyes, the routine choreography appeared nothing short of masterful. We all threw ourselves into it like we had been waiting our whole lives for that moment.

Step touch, step touch, clap your hands, turn around, slide and pose.

We gave it our all and high-fived each other every time we repeated it.

With our spirits high and the room moving in unison, Abuti Ben asked us all to sit in a circle and wait to see another style of dance that they wanted to introduce to us – Latin and ballroom dancing. He explained that they would demonstrate it, as it could not be readily explained and required years of technical training and discipline. Then off they went to change. Moments later, they emerged. Ausi Mpho was adorned in a pink tulle ballroom dress, with a sweetheart neckline, and Abuti Ben in a black, sequined tail jacket, a white shirt, a bow tie, black trousers, black socks and black shoes.

Even before they made their first move to the initial beat, I was entranced by the sequined tail jacket. Then the music began, and they swayed, slid, twisted and turned with an elegance I had never seen before. The tail jacket shimmered as the light caught the sequins. The room was quiet as we watched them glide across the floor; you could hear a pin drop. That was the first time I had ever witnessed ballroom dancing. It was graceful, as though they were floating, suspended above the floor. Their timing and the ease with which they synchronised their every move was thrilling.

Shortly afterwards, I walked up to Abuti Ben.

'Where can I get a jacket like that?' I asked, my voice faltering.

He flashed me a knowing smile.

'You had better come back tomorrow and learn how to dance, and then maybe, one day, you'll get to wear a sequined tail jacket like this.'

I was sold. At the next practice time, I was back. I would keep returning, even as other people began to drop out. We had fun with it, but the training was tough, and the recreation hall was not meant for dancing. The floor was cement, and I think that is why my knees are still busted to this day. The room was either too cold or so hot that we would have sweat pouring down our backs as we danced. It was unforgiving.

This programme was the first of its kind and, after the weekend trial session, it ran every weekday between 3pm and 5pm. No one was paying Abuti Ben and Ausi Mpho, but it was their passion, and it was starting to become mine too.

Often, I watched dance shows on the TV at home. I would sit, my eyes glued to the screen.

'Bedtime, Baba. It's late,' Mum would say, putting her arm around me.

'Please,' I would plead, even though I could feel the heavy weight of my eyelids desperate to close.

'No, it's too late. I will record it.'

Not long after the TV came to our house, it was joined by a VCR video recorder, meaning I could record my dance shows and watch them obsessively in every spare moment that I had away from school and dance practice.

The beauty of that time was that, as a child growing up in the township, you typically had a variety of activities that you could be a part of courtesy of community projects like the one Ausi Mpho and Abuti Ben were running. There was football, rugby, boxing, tennis, drama and, now, Latin American and ballroom dance. But, gradually, most of the youngsters dropped out to try something new. First, the boys who didn't fancy the sequined jackets and had shown up just for the girls started to fade out; then, others who realised that learning ballroom and Latin required hours of learning basic steps on repeat began to thin out too. It required precise footwork and dedication. So soon we were down to six from a group of more than fifty children and teenagers.

The three boys left were paired with the three remaining girls according to height. In the crowd was Abuti, one of my friends who went to the same school. He was a year above me and one of the most caring people I knew. I was drawn to him. He wasn't bothered by my energy, gestures or how I would twirl in the street after dance classes. Instead, he seemed fascinated by me and wanted to hang out and see what I got up to outside of school.

Initially, I was somewhat disappointed because I had hoped to be paired with him.

'Why can't boys dance with boys?' I asked Abuti Ben.

'It simply doesn't work that way in the world of ballroom,' he replied. 'You will be partnered with a girl. That's just how it works.'

Hearing my exchange with Abuti Ben, Modiehi, the girl I was paired with, was outraged.

'It's fine if you don't want to dance with me,' she said, shrugging her shoulders. I could tell she was hurt.

'No, no,' I backtracked. 'It's not that. I invited Abuti because I had hoped we could be paired together.'

She seemed perplexed by this. Abuti Ben defused the situation and told us that Modiehi and I would be dancing with each other. Full stop. Abuti would be paired with one of the other girls. Modiehi and I smiled reluctantly at each other. Unbeknown to us then, we would go on to do well together. It was the beginning of a wonderful partnership – despite a rocky start.

Shortly after that, Abuti stopped coming to dance. He dropped out to play sports like most of the other boys, but we remained good friends. It was easy to see why the novelty wore off because, even though we were training hard, it was hard to imagine what might be beyond it. As far as we could see, there was nowhere to go with it. One of the ways that I stayed motivated was that Ausi Mpho stayed on my street, so if I missed practice, she would always come to our house.

'He wasn't there. Where was he and what was he doing?' she would ask Mum.

I also loved to watch children dancing in talent shows on TV and adults in professional dance shows. I never believed I could be like them, but it kept me returning to the recreation hall each week. I wanted to have some sparkles in my life.

About a year into training, I was told we were ready for our first competition. I always relished the opportunity to leave the township. It often meant new clothes, a trip on the minibus and seeing new places.

My mum and the other parents took some convincing: it cost money and we were not going to win anything, so they couldn't see the benefit.

We never had any money until the end of the month when Dad was paid, so Ausi Mpho and Abuti Ben agreed to pay for me, and my family would pay them back. The costume was another matter; I needed black trousers, black shoes, a white shirt, a cummerbund (South Africans call it a cummer belt) and a bow tie. The first three items were taken care of because they were the same as my school uniform. We then searched around the township to find a cummerbund, and somebody produced just what I needed from the back of a cupboard somewhere.

Modiehi's mum had a bit more money than most of us and

went all the way to Johannesburg to get her a princess dress. It was not dance-worthy because the material was wrong, and it was not cut like a dancer's dress because she had picked it off the rail in an ordinary shop. What I know now is that dresses at that level need to be plain with a matching Lycra leotard top and skirt, but hers was far too elaborate and covered in diamanté crystals – a firm no-no for beginner dancers like us. Either way, Modiehi definitely looked like a princess. We said we would take our food with us in Tupperware and, by the time we left, we had been given enough food to last us an entire week because everyone cooked for us. At least we could eat like kings.

The excitement as we packed up a minibus to drive to Bophelong, a township about thirty minutes from Zamdela, was obvious; I couldn't stop grinning.

These types of competitions were designed for township communities and dance clubs. It meant that everyone could compete without having to travel across the country. It was all run on a slight shoestring to make it more affordable for every-one, and the hall would be hired out in the evening to cut costs. The competition started at around 6pm. I was taking part in the juvenile bronze section, the most junior level of competition. After our class, it moved to juvenile silver and juvenile gold, then to juniors and up the ages until the adults danced long into the night.

As we walked in, I was blown away by the masses of dancers from neighbouring towns who had the same passion as me, spinning and cha-cha-cha-ing across the floor. There must have been more than a hundred dancers there, and many of them had their parents doing their hair or tying up their laces at the side of the floor. The sun was still high in the sky, and it cast a warm glow across the hall. When the music started, the dancers were carried into a world defined by rhythm and grace. Their feet moved in sync, executing intricate steps with prowess. It was a tableau of swirling colours.

There were family members everywhere and all the local people came to cheer on their loved ones. There was this incredible sense of togetherness, even though we were competing against one another. It was as though a whole new world had opened up before me. Now, I could see beyond the four walls of the recreation centre and the dusty streets of Zamdela.

When our class was announced a few minutes after arriving, we raced to prepare. I had no expectations and took Modiehi's hand, and we started our steps as we had been taught.

We had been practising our cha-cha-cha and jive routines for a couple of weeks. There was always so much to remember and take in that we gave our steps different names that we would whisper to each other to keep ourselves on track and the dance moving. We named our steps after animals – the horse or tiger – things we could see; or feelings, like 'fly me to the moon'.

We started dancing to The Beatles' 'Twist and Shout'; I remember that routine like it was yesterday. Adrenalin coursed through me as I felt my tummy crackle with excitement. I felt sick; a nervous feeling that never went away, whatever the competition. We exploded into action. One of our dances was the jive. With each flick of the leg, kick and bounce, the noise from the crowd seemed to get louder. I used to do a step where I shook my shoulders and rotated around my partner while she stood still. As I did this move, waves of delight rippled through the crowd.

Shortly after, we were called up to the judges' table and told we were disqualified. It turned out that this shoulder move was an advanced move only meant for higher levels and not entry-level dancers. We didn't really study the ins and outs of what was or was not allowed during training. It was always just about fun.

There was no disappointment. I could not care less that we did not make it through because I was just so thrilled by the experience.

We slept in the hall under blankets. No one does competitions the way that South African townships do; it was a make-do environment, and someone provided a pillow and blankets, and we would take one and find a space to settle down for the night. While Modiehi slept quietly next to me, her eyelids fluttering with dreams, I stayed awake and watched all the other dancers, who were so captivating and elegant with upright postures – gliding, swirling and twirling in sync with the music. Their expressions radiated joy and passion, and their movements were so fluid that it seemed they moved like water.

I also discovered how revered Ausi Mpho and Abuti Ben were. We never saw them train because, when we left the hall, their rehearsals started. They were heavyweights in the dance sport community. When their number was called and they took to the floor, I was shocked to see some other would-be dancers step off with defeated sighs as they knew they stood no chance against them. It was a moment to behold as they started dancing. They were adorned in the most beautiful gold costumes. They were a wonder; every movement and gesture conveyed their deep connection and love of ballroom dancing. Their bodies seemed to meld together in perfect harmony. In my mind, it was like they had transcended dance into something even bigger.

'You are trained by the best,' onlookers told me. 'Just look at them. They are icons.'

I was exhausted and, eventually, I gave in to the fatigue. I fell asleep to the beats of the music and the sound of the turns, spins and dips just inches from me, with a smile resting on my lips.

On our return home the next day, Ausi Mpho rushed to her home to give us old trophies so we could pretend to our families that we had won something. She wanted us to show them these so that they would continue to let us train. She couldn't bear the idea of our parents saying: 'But you didn't even win, and we've had to spend all this money.' There needed to be some return on going off for the weekend and the money they had spent.

Ausi Mpho gave me a small gold trophy, but I was honest with my mum.

'Mummy, I did an advanced step, and that's why I was disqualified. And Modiehi's dress – it was not good. We are learning a new syllabus now. Next time, we will win,' I said, hopefully. She seemed to accept this.

The kids in my township felt like they were already on the back foot because they didn't have the money to match up to other dancers. There was an ingrained sense of inequality and, with that, a struggle to understand what the ultimate goal could or would be. It was a world we were discovering was not built for Black township boys and girls from our backgrounds. The costs required to continue participating in competitions were exorbitant for our families. I was growing out of my shoes quicker than an infant.

From the six of us left in the dance club, it was eventually just me and Modiehi who remained. However, Abuti Ben and Ausi Mpho were not deterred. They gave us every ounce of their time and attention. They never missed a single session. There were times when Abuti Ben would leave the tavern with an unfinished bottle of beer in hand to make it in time. But conversely, they gave us no room for lateness or not showing up with our A-game. They taught us the basics of the samba, cha-cha-cha, rumba, paso doble and, my favourite, the jive. The more they taught us, the more we wanted to drink from their well of knowledge. While I had talked to Mum about a syllabus, training did not follow strict patterns of learning steps and repeating them to death. Abuti Ben and Ausi Mpho came up with inventive ways of always making it exciting and enjoyable – they would mix up steps and routines to keep it interesting for us. We were young, and it kept our attention.

Despite challenges raising funds for entries, costumes, dance shoes and transportation, Modiehi and I moved up in the Latin and ballroom world. We slowly began to understand that our commitment to the craft would be our saving grace. We would compensate for our lack of extravagant costumes by working twice as hard to win over the judges with our technique and talent. Every time we hit the dance floor, we understood that we had to push ourselves harder and dance ourselves to the ground.

Abuti Ben used to hype us up. He convinced us that we could be world champions. At that point, we didn't understand what that was or what it meant. He would continually tell us that we were the best in the world. His affirmations charged our determination. From that age, I understood that dancing brought me joy and fulfilment, and my goal was to be the South African champion and win the World Championship. Abuti Ben gave us the tools to dare to win. Did I truly believe him that anything was possible? No, I don't think so, but I kept going. The reason I didn't believe his words? There was always a disconnect. Even at that age, I didn't see how I could exist in that world and rise to the top when we didn't have the resources to do so. I never allowed myself to dream that I would ever really make it and lift international trophies high above my head anywhere other than in my mind. But I loved dancing, I had dreams, and that was enough.

Dancing also became my second home. While I was bullied at school and felt like I didn't belong in the unforgiving streets of my township, in the dance world, I was in a safe space. It was a place where even the straight boys wore outfits adorned with crystals, styled their hair and looked conspicuously camp in tight vests and black trousers. It was a competitive world on the dance floor and an inclusive one off it.

As I started to train more, my practices bled late in the evening as I watched the adults rehearse. At those times, the recreation centre was always a place for anyone who loved to dance and the gay community, young and old, would come together to move their bodies in a way that felt natural to them. No one had to alter their physicality or speech. Now, it is clear to me that many people used the space as a refuge.

Abuti Ben would always tell me to stand tall and proud and never shy away from being present.

'Bryan Watson doesn't slouch!' Abuti Ben laughed, referring to the much-celebrated South African Latin Dance champion. 'Carry yourself like a dancer.' I would automatically stand two inches taller. It was ingrained into me that being a dancer was a way of life – you couldn't just forget about it when you went home.

As soon as I left the recreation centre to go home, it was a lonely road and I was vulnerable to bullies. So, as I got a bit older and when the dancing had finished for the evening, I would wait for Ausi Mpho so we could walk home together. It always felt safer that way. Sometimes, when Ausi Mpho was going out after dance practice, she would hand me her bag and ask me to take it to her house. Instead, I would bring it to our home. Away from prying eyes and before I returned Ausi Mpho's bag to her the following day, I would sometimes take out her dancing shoes and parade around the house in them. She had yellow sandals from a popular woman's shop called Miladys, which I would wear until Mum chided me, warning that she would not be responsible for replacing them if I broke them. She told me she would not be breaking into our grocery budget just because I wanted to gyrate in heels.

* * *

Due to finances, we had to discount attending many of the competitions, but there were certain qualifying competitions that we could not miss. To progress, we needed to see how we would fare on a bigger stage.

When I was around ten, my first major competition took me to Johannesburg City Hall. Johannesburg is a city on a level with London, New York, Paris and Berlin – big cities with lights and tall buildings, where big stars come to shine. The furthest I had ever been out of our township was to Vereeniging and Vanderbijlpark, towns 31 kilometres or so from home where I would go Christmas clothes shopping with my parents, so I was travelling further than ever before. I knew it was a definitive moment for me. I was dancing in the novice section in a competition, and no expense would be spared. The competition would be during the day, and I would be dancing alongside everyone.

My mum could not contain her pride and joy, telling everybody her son was competing with Modiehi there. Word quickly got around, and Abuti Ben and Ausi Mpho collected money to help fund our trip. Someone volunteered their van to drive us, and we had enough money for the entry fees and better clothing. What was most exciting was that we were prepared to be seen. We had trained so, so hard.

The journey was long – around 90 kilometres – and it was the first time I had been to the megacity. We all crammed into that bus and joked and laughed our way there. There was never pressure from our trainers, but always just so much fun, both on and off the dance floor. My belief in the success of any dance or partnership is when your energy matches. However hard we worked to get our technique or choreography right, it was only when we were laughing and enjoying ourselves that the magic happened. When our energy was in sync, a transformation took place.

Stepping into the hall, I felt like I was walking into a palace. It was a neoclassical style with a grand and ornate façade with intricate detailing. It set the stage for a night of incredible performances, but I could already tell that there was new scrutiny that focused on grooming and technique. For the first time, I was competing against dancers from all other races and cultures. I had never before seen such a mixture of ethnicities together in one room. It felt more competitive than our previous competitions and, while people cheered each other on, it was clear that all the dancers were there to win.

There was evidence of money everywhere, from the way people spoke to the way their dresses clung to or hung from their bodies. So many of the other dancers possessed this unique confidence that comes from having more and being seen as 'more than'. Everything we lacked was amplified.

We had a sequence of dances prepared, including the cha-cha-cha and the jive again. I remember the nerves, but also nailing our routines and knowing we had done well. We moved seamlessly between dance styles to the delighted faces of our trainers. While we did not have the resources of other dancers, what we lacked in costumes, we made up for in training time and, importantly, the stamina and strength that came with those hundreds of hours of sweat and laughter. We were young, but from the second we got onto the dance floor to the moment we left it, we gave it every ounce of energy we had. It was like a switch had been flicked on; we propelled ourselves along, ignited with the desire to do well.

Abuti Ben used to say to us: 'You have to step outside of your-self to perform.' That day, I plastered on a smile over my nerves and followed his advice.

As we made it through the rounds, I could see everyone was on a level playing field. I was starting to look around me and see the competition. It was unspoken that some dancers were better than others, and I knew we were being seen. The place buzzed with energy as dancers and their partners mingled and exchanged words of encouragement. All classes and colours blended together.

The announcement of who was in the final was on a sheet in the hallway of the venue. There was no way that Modiehi or I could get to the front as everyone was clambering around to see. I remember Abuti Ben shouting, 'You made it, you made it,' and hugging us.

When Modiehi and I danced again in the finals, we had to wait for the announcement of the winners over the loudspeakers. There were seven couples dancing and six places. The other names were called painfully slowly.

When it wheeled up to second place and our name still had not been called, I resigned myself to seventh place. That was fine; it had been an experience.

'And in first place, couple number eleven.'

It was our number. My jaw hit the floor; I was gobsmacked. Then, I cried like a baby. I sobbed and sobbed tears of happiness that mingled with the sweat of the day. Our trainers and the people around us celebrated the win as if it were their own, lifting us high on to their shoulders and hollering.

Later, as we stood on the podium clutching our beautiful trophy, Ausi Mpho said to me: 'Now don't ever step off that podium, Johannes. That is where you belong.'

It was too late to go to bed that night, so we slept in the van while other competitors wheeled their suitcases off to nearby lavish hotels. It did not matter. We had won. It was my first real taste of success and, boy, it tasted so sweet.

I returned home the next day to find my mother looking out for me at the gate of the home. News must have got to her. As soon as I saw her figure approaching me, I lifted the trophy and ran down the street, waving it above my head. Like a scene from a Bollywood film, my mum charged towards me, lifted me on her back like she did when I was a baby, and paraded down the street, ululating. She had me supported with one hand on her back and the trophy proudly raised with the other hand. She was bursting with joy and pride.

Some of our neighbours came out, and the moment turned into a mini street party. There was music and food and dancing. Until then, I had never felt that I was part of my community in that way. The affirmation that moment offered me reinforced that I represented a community of people who needed me to win. They were deeply proud. You never fully realise how your win is everyone's win until the community rises to celebrate victory. I often marvel at the support and pride great artists, athletes and leaders elicit. It reminds us that we are connected in ways we often downplay.

As the weeks rolled around, I found that dance was endearing me to my community in a way that afforded me some small level of affection and value and, therefore, a greater sense of safety and protection. The threats were still there, but the more word spread that we represented the community at dance competitions, the more tolerant people appeared to become – the more I felt championed for my talent rather than berated for how I spoke or moved. My friends and I could walk in our shortest shorts more confidently, knowing some community members would protect us. I was still called names, but you would hear women say, 'Leave those children alone,' to the unrelenting bullies.

I started to understand where I was in the food chain of South African life, but as Abuti Ben said: 'Your situation cannot stop you from being great.'

Dance had become a trusted friend, and I never looked back.

Chapter Three

Locked Out

When I was eleven, my grandmother Mme passed away. She had heart issues. I recall her feet swelling and people talking about her going to the hospital as if she had already died. When anyone went to the hospital, it would never be good news.

This was the first time I experienced the true ruin of death. As in many African families, my grandmother was not just the matriarch, but a woman my sister and I considered a maternal figure, perhaps even more so than our mother. Coming back from school, she would be the smiling face I would find waiting for me. I knew that a hot meal would be coming. She was my comfort and constant confidante. She was the closest thing I had to a friend in my early childhood, so being made to walk past her open coffin to pay my respects is a moment that will always haunt me.

'Say goodbye to your granny,' I was told. I did not want to remember her like that.

Her void in my life felt huge and permeated my soul.

We did not anticipate what a dark shadow Mme's passing would leave behind, even on the sunniest of days. After his mother's death, my father's drinking grew increasingly worse.

He had started drinking openly after his father's passing, but because his mother lived with us, it was under control. The only incident I remember when his drinking got out of hand was when he locked us all out of the house for the first time. I remember hearing him slurring his words and periodically snoring. Mme banged the door and admonished him for hours until he eventually opened up.

Before her passing, I lived a very protected life and, between my granny and Mum, the home was a haven. But in the days that followed her death, home no longer felt like a fun place. When Dad's drinking got worse, he began mistreating Mum. My father would never physically harm her, but instead acted cruelly in the way he spoke to her, telling her that he did not love her anymore.

This was a challenging time in my young life and I struggled to understand it all. I understood that my dad loved me and my sister dearly; there was no doubt about that. We also loved him without compromise. But I couldn't comprehend how my mother suddenly could not be afforded that same love and affection. It was as though she had become an outlet for my father to exorcise his demons and, I suppose, his grief. During the week, we would have our lovely father and my mum would have her husband. Then, come Friday night, the monster would rear its head. I would wait with bated breath to have my father back at the start of the new week.

My dance routine provided an anchor in this storm. Not long after our win in Johannesburg, Modiehi decided she wanted to give up dancing. I could not understand it. We had only just started, but she was interested in doing other things, like hanging out with her friends and boys. She had so much talent that it would go to waste. I almost walked away from dancing myself because I felt so disappointed.

'You must know a girl willing to do this?' my trainers asked.

I started trying to recruit other children in school and the streets around my home.

'There is a world that you guys will love,' I would say, approaching groups in the playground or near the house. I would tell them about the world of dance.

'We go to competitions. We go to Sun City.'

Sun City is a luxury resort in the North West province of South Africa, known for its entertainment, restaurants, bars and casinos. It sounded almost as good as Disneyland.

'Really?' They were sceptical.

In the end, a girl called Magauta Matena started to come to my training sessions. She was my height and had long, beautiful legs. Magauta was timid and did not say a lot, but she was a very quick learner and soaked up information and new steps like a sponge.

Abuti Ben and Ausi Mpho were determined.

'Don't worry. We will get her to the standard she needs to be,' they told me.

Initially, it felt quite frustrating to train with a novice, but she had the right attitude and was keen to learn. She was different. Very quickly, she was able to dance as well as Modiehi. We made it work and started winning every competition that we entered in our province. We were the team to beat. But when we stepped outside of our province, we found it harder. Again, the issue of not having the right resources loomed heavily in the background.

I loathed going to compete on weekends because my mother and Jabulile would be left alone to deal with whatever my father would subject them to that weekend. My sister would often end up in an open confrontation with Dad in defence of Mum. Aside from those times, my sister had a strong relationship with Dad – he adored Jabu and me.

In addition to alcohol, my father's other weakness was women. As a boy, I remember eavesdropping on multiple conversations between my aunt and mother about my father's infidelity.

During one of our regular football outings, not long after that dance competition in Johannesburg, I witnessed the extent of my father's cheating. One Saturday, after his team, Kaizer Chiefs, had played a match, my father convinced me that it was too late to catch a minibus taxi home that night, so we had to sleep in another township, Sharpeville, at the house of his 'friend'. I was confused because it was clear that my father was lying. The sun had not set and there appeared to be plenty of minibuses waiting on the streets with eager drivers beckoning passengers to board. I nodded and held tightly on to his hand, trusting that we would eventually make it home safely together the following day. We slept at one of his lady friend's houses that night. It was one of the women I would often see him and some of his other friends with at the stadium.

Initially, I didn't think anything of her because I knew her as one of my dad's friends. The group also tagged along to her house, so it seemed innocent enough. The only warning sign was getting to her house and feeling homesick, like an emptiness in my tummy. I wanted to be home and not surrounded by drunk adults being raucous. We had gone from a loud stadium of cheering fans to an after-party of older men and women speaking over each other to a soundtrack of loud music. At some point, I fell asleep on the sofa and was eventually carried to one of the bedrooms. I woke up calling out for my father in the middle of the night. I walked around the now quiet house, littered with empty drinks bottles and a cloying stench of cigarettes. Finally, I ended up in the main bedroom, where I found my father passed out next to this lady. Something inside of me was revolted. Then, I decided not to be an accessory to Dad's adultery. Out of respect for my mum, I climbed into the bed and, eventually, fell asleep. Whatever plans they had, nothing would happen on my watch. The three of us slept together until the morning.

After we had woken up and left, my father made me swear I would not mention last night's shenanigans to my mother.

'Don't say anything to Mum. You must not tell her.'

I nodded in agreement. Not only was I disappointed in my father, but I was seething. The first thing I did as soon as we got home and opened the door, was to spew out that we had spent the night at the home of one of my father's lady friends.

'Daddy shared a bed with a woman,' I said. 'He said there were no taxis coming, so we had to sleep at her house.'

My mum's expression betrayed nothing.

'Baba, go and get ready for school,' she instructed, and I left the room. I don't remember ever seeing my father that defeated – it was in the angle of his head as it hung down.

I have no idea what got into my head that day, but I needed to be honest. I owed it to my mother. It was no secret that I was mummy's boy.

I knew I was taking a major risk that could mean my father would never trust me again. Or that we would never go on our weekend escapades to the stadium again. At that moment, I was convinced that it was a risk that I was willing to take for my father to be the type of husband my mother deserved. In my little head, it was as simple as that. You are caught; there's some form of justice and lesson learned, never to be repeated. As much as I got on well with my father, I was disappointed in him for putting me in such a difficult position.

Shortly after this, my sister moved out. While Mum's response to my dad's cheating and occasional cruel outbursts was silence, Jabu would confront him. It reached the point where it was no longer healthy for them to be under the same roof. I know he would never have raised his hand to her, but she hated his behaviour and was so unhappy being around it all the time. So Jabu moved in with my aunt, my mum's older sister Martha.

Through all the conversations I would eavesdrop on about my father's ways, my heart always felt heavy for my mum. As young as I was, I knew she was a good woman and my father was fortunate to have her. However, I didn't think she deserved to be treated so poorly. She didn't deserve all the turmoil and heartache.

I grew more and more protective of my mother. Children are pretty perceptive. It was clear to me who was in the wrong. I just wanted to equip my mother with enough proof to reassure her that she was not delusional or imagining my father's behaviour.

I did not know just how pervasive my father's infidelities were. One day, we received an unwelcome guest at our front door. An angry man was banging on the door, looking for Dad. My father was out drinking. The now furious caller slipped a note under the door explaining that the woman with whom my father was having an affair was his partner. He was unprepared to take this lying down and sought to hit my father where it hurt most. It was clear he had come for us, Dad's family, to get back at him. My mum and I sat in silence for a while. Then, after what felt like an impossibly long time, I took the letter from my mother and read it aloud.

'You will pay for what you have done,' it read.

We were all frightened that night. It was in the way he banged on our door and came through the gate with white-knuckled fury. I knew that it could quickly spill into violence.

Around that time, I told Mum that Dad had gone too far. Reflecting on the reassurance she had provided me years before, I assured her that she was loved and capable, even without my father. She didn't have to stick around for our sake. This was hard to admit, as I loved my dad dearly. However, I realised it was just as important for my mother to escape the situation because I no longer felt theirs was a loving relationship. My father had become unrecognisable, his behaviour increasingly difficult to bear. As Dad continued to taunt Mum, saying the love was gone and even playing the Teddy Pendergrass song, 'I Don't Love You Anymore' on repeat, the light went out in her eyes. She seemed a shadow of her former self, shuffling around the house, taking his words without complaint, and then going to bed.

Alcohol abuse was bringing out the worst in my father. I still believe that his drinking led to all of the pain and, eventually, my parent's separation. I think he wanted to force my mum out of the house so that she would leave and the responsibility for the breakdown of their marriage would somehow be shared. As a child, I couldn't wrap my head around it. On the one hand, my father was a loving provider and parent, but on the other, he could be an abusive alcoholic. I have gained far more understanding as I have grown older. I now understand that he was a young man trying to figure out life. I see now that alcoholism is an illness for which most people need intensive support to overcome and heal. The beauty of growing up is that I have begun to understand these things better. I have developed empathy and try to be non-judgemental.

I continued to dance each night after school and compete at the weekends. There was no space for self-pity or wallowing in life's disappointments. There were too many to process as a community, let alone whatever might happen in our families and personal lives. If we allowed that to take over, we would never survive or make our way. We were treated like adults who were expected to not bring moods into the room.

'When you walk into this room, forget about what worries you,' Abuti Ben told us. 'Don't bring whatever it is that you carry with you into this room. Let it go at the door.'

Abuti Ben told us that, when we were training in the recreation hall, it was a 'sacred space', and we respected that. We are a dancing nation. I was taught to dance when I was happy, sad or across a whole gamut of emotions.

For a long time, Aunt Martha was the only person trying to convince my mother to walk away from the abuse. My mum and aunt were part of a family of ten and, of all the siblings, they were the closest. Though they had different temperaments and personalities, they were best friends with fierce female loyalty. My auntie was the fire, and my mother the water that doused the flames. Mum had chosen to be a housewife, while my aunt decided to study to become a nurse. My Aunt Martha was the first of her siblings to buy her own house without the help of a man. She was kind, smart and strong; a woman who wore her heart on her sleeve. Other than my sister Jabu, my aunt was the only other person who could take on my father on my mum's behalf. There were times when Auntie would come to our house to confront my father about his ill treatment of my mother. She was ready to tackle him and throw a punch if it came to that.

One time, word got around that Dad was involved with a particular woman in the township. Blame it on boredom, but like any small town, the people of Zamdela tend to know each other's business.

One day, my aunt and mum took me with them to the woman's home. When we arrived, I saw a side to my mum and aunt that I didn't know existed. They were gunning for my father. After screaming and yelling for him to leave his mistress' locked house, she eventually peered through a window and threatened to call the police. My father, who was clearly inside, refused to come out. Defeated but undeterred, the two sisters went home.

That night, my aunt insisted on waiting until my father eventually returned. Dad publicly humiliated Mum, and my aunt would not sit idly by as her sister was turned into a laughing stock. Dad did not return until the early hours, but when he did, he awoke a rage in my aunt. She brought him to his knees, telling him off in a way I had never seen anyone speak to him before. I felt so overprotective that I went to sit next to my father on the edge of the bed. It was my way of reassuring him that I was there for him. It was a strange gesture of loyalty because, even then, I knew that my aunt was right to challenge him. But as he faced the music for his poor choices, part of me wanted to shield him and I knew my presence would defuse the situation. It was always like that with my father. After a blow-up like that, peace would be restored until the demons returned. It was an anxious wait for the next incident. While we would be grateful for the peace, we could never really enjoy it because of the dread of what could come next.

Sometimes, after a long session, Dad would absurdly yell at us to get out of his house. Voices would be raised, threats made, and sometimes they would shove each other until Mum was pushed outside. On those nights, I would follow my mother outside in solidarity, and we would huddle under the stars until my father came back to his senses.

My mother's departure from the family home was a long time coming. It took time before she heeded everyone's counsel. On the fateful day, we returned from visiting my Aunt Martha to find the house locked from the inside. Dad repeatedly shouted that we should go back to where we came from. We sat by the back door and waited. When my father eventually opened it, an altercation ensued. Mum had always said that the day my father raised his hand to her would be the last day of their marriage. Dad tried to slap Mum in the face, and she ducked but bumped into the sharp corner of the stove as she attempted to dodge him. It must have been the impact or the blood gushing from her face, but she called out for me, and we ran until we got to my aunt's house. Mum never looked back. The scar remained on her face for weeks, a bitter reminder of the episode.

Mum did not hesitate to move in with her sister when the time came, and my aunt had long reassured her that we were welcome. She, along with her two boys, told my mother to bring her children. They would make room for all of us. My auntie lived in a much better neighbourhood where the houses were slightly bigger. The area was called Success. It was a new district built for young professionals, among whom there were teachers, medics and civil servants. Each house was designed, uniquely for the time, with inside toilets and multiple bedrooms – a far cry from the four-room houses built for Black families during Apartheid, which only had two small bedrooms.

The next time my mother went back to our house, it was to collect her possessions. My aunt organised a van, and we all went to get our clothes and my mum's bedding. I was devastated and put my arm around my dad before he stormed out. I knew that the blame lay squarely on his shoulders, but I felt an unswerving loyalty towards him and guilt that we were leaving. We slowly packed the van. My mum left my father with enough furniture to live on, but took anything sentimental for her. As we made our way back to my aunt's house, we drove past my father on his way back to the house. I don't know where he had been, but he was so intoxicated that he didn't even see us.

Steadily, my Aunt Martha became my everything and the one person in my family I consistently looked up to. I admire her drive and strength as much now as I did back then. With her strong personality, my aunt's superpowers came from how deeply she loved and cared for people. She was the kind to fight for the people in whom she believed. While mum was a softly-spoken, gentle soul who loved peace at all costs, my auntie was ready to go to war for her values. And yet, somehow, the two sisters loved each other in a way I still marvel at. Their total loyalty and sisterhood were unbreakable.

I immediately felt at home in my auntie's home. I loved living in this warm environment, even if it meant sharing a room with my sister and mother. We were well taken care of. My auntie's salary as a nurse took care of all our needs, including some money to enter dance competitions and school fees. The fees that went to school were not much but paid for books and stationery. For the children who walked for miles to get to school in bare feet because they could not afford shoes, there was an understanding that their parents would 'pay later' to save their pride. I became quite proficient at sewing and had progressed from my Barbie dolls to letting down the hems of my trousers and making one set of clothing last much longer than it might've done otherwise.

Mum faced joblessness for a spell and I recalled that, for a long time, she had expressed regrets about her life and never realised her dream of becoming a teacher. Dad had refused her the joy of pursuing it and, as the years went by, I imagine she lost confidence in her dream. Looking at my mother and how patient and disciplined she is, I can only imagine what a good teacher she could have been. I used to wonder what could have become of my mother had her dreams been nurtured. I applaud her courage to put her aspirations aside, trust somebody to look after her and raise us as devotedly as she did.

Shortly after we moved in with my aunt, Dad moved another woman into our former home. She was not someone I knew, and she already had a son who moved in with her. I remember once walking into Zamdela and passing the house. She stood outside.

'Your father is not here,' she told me in a cold voice. Behind her was the home that I had known and loved, but it was no longer a place where I felt welcome.

In under three years, I had gone from dealing with the pain of losing my grandmother to watching my parents' marriage dissolve. My friends and my dancing remained my respite. I stuck close to Seun and Jeff. Dancing was something that was mine and spoke to me. In our friendship trio, we had all fallen upon something we loved. Jeff used to play netball. Defying tradition and playing for the school's team, he was the only boy. He became a phenomenon. No one could touch him, and he was skilled, brilliant and unrivalled in the sport. Then there was Seun, who loved reading and music. He was undoubtedly the brains of the group. I felt so fortunate to have such excellent friends. At our school, we were taught in Sesotho. None of the teachers addressed us in English unless it was for English class. Seun wanted us to learn to read and speak English fluently and insisted that reading was fundamental. He would carry magazines and notebooks peppered with English lyrics for us to go through. After school, we would be locked in my room learning English from the US top 10, where we would write down the lyrics to the songs as they came on the radio. While Jeff threw himself into sport and essentially became a star athlete, and Seun forced us to level up on our education, I danced as if my life depended on it.

We always found time for the three of us to hang out together. We called ourselves 'Destiny's Child', after the iconic US pop group. After school, we would sing and dance to their tunes and fight over who would be Beyoncé that day. Seun would usually win because I was never confident enough to push myself to the front.

We didn't know that while these pop groups were inspiring us, somewhere in South Africa another trio of boys would later emerge as the country's first openly gay pop group. 3Sum, fronted by Amstel Maboa, alongside Koyo Bala and Jeff Moyo, was one of South Africa's most talked about bands of the early noughties. Made up of three openly out and vibrant gay men, 3Sum epitomised the dawn of our country's new beginning.

They were unapologetically gay, loud and proud. Jeff, Seun and I lost our minds, singing and dancing along to their tunes. 3Sum was not so much a band that we loved because of its artistry or music but because of the validation that the band afforded us. We felt represented, visible and affirmed, and finally felt a sense of belonging, especially in the public domain. We idolised 3Sum and everything that they represented. Through them, we, too, thought that we could share in celebrating South Africa's new and much-celebrated constitution. From a country that had faced global sanctions for its decades-long human rights violations, South Africa had emerged as a country on the way up, with one of the finest constitutions in the world. It was lauded for its human rights framework. That moment allowed us to celebrate being born in a country where our rights were now exalted and sanctified. Over the years, Jeff, Seun and I would fight to define our space by wearing our shorts quite short and through our numerous failed attempts at starting a band. If 3Sum could boldly claim their spot in the world, so could we.

Chapter Four

For Whom the Bell Tolls

Aunt Martha's home was my home for the remainder of my time at primary school and the start of my dancing career. Dance had never been a language that was fluently spoken in my home. Football? Yes. Dance? No. Despite this, my mum remained supportive throughout all my years of learning to dance. She was not, however, a typical 'dance mum', cheering on and screaming from the stands. There were plenty of those types of women at the competitions we went to. To sit and watch me for hours on end at dance practice was not my mum's idea of a relaxing evening. Instead, she was the kind of mum who would ensure my costumes were washed and ironed, shoes polished and lunches packed for out-of-town competitions. Fuss-free, some might call it, and never over the top.

As overbearing as Mum could be when it came to school, she was a softer touch when it came to dance training. Some nights, I trained so late that I would stay overnight at the recreation hall under a spare blanket, and she allowed me to do this, confident that I was being looked after. I got used to not having my family physically present at many tournaments. I understood and saw how much they sacrificed for me, scraping together what they could so I could attend competitions. I didn't expect there would be enough money for them to be able to attend all of my competitions, but I knew that I had the full support of both my mum and auntie, and they would do all they could to help me follow my dreams. I am profoundly grateful to have had these two women who backed me at a time when dancing wasn't seen as a sensible sport or viable career prospect.

I always loved looking smart during dance training and at school. At Tsatsi Primary, I made history as the first student to be commended as the 'best-dressed learner', an award meant to encourage students to take pride in dressing neatly in their school uniform. Mum, to whom I owed the win, beamed with pride. She ensured I was always pristinely dressed and never missed a day of school, however late I had been training the night before. It was an unspoken agreement that, whatever was happening with my dance, schoolwork and trying hard in my studies needed to be a constant.

Most days, I would be home late, but I couldn't let my schoolwork slip and my mum would tell me that I needed to do my homework. I would wake up gritty-eyed the next morning, exhausted but ready to go to school and do it all again.

For many years, my life revolved around those two worlds: school and dance. At school, I was shy and reserved because of the bullying and my discomfort being queer in a straight environment. All I ever wanted was to be ordinary or at least to have the opportunity to exist peacefully in the background. As a result, I was obsessed with avoiding anything that could draw attention to me. I stayed out of trouble and kept unnecessary attention to a minimum until the end of grade five, when my life as I knew it changed in ways I could have never anticipated.

One day, without warning, I was summoned to the head teacher's office, where I can still vividly recall my palms becoming clammy and beads of sweat trickling down the sides of my head. I knew that the only time anyone was called to the principal's office was for bad news. My mind raced as I contemplated how my mum would react if I got into trouble. She had made it crystal clear from early on that she would not tolerate being called to the school because of my behaviour and that she expected me to be an exemplary student.

This was reinforced every day in the way Mum insisted I return home from school as immaculately clean as I had left that morning. No strand of hair could be out of place and my shoes had to be wiped with balled-up tights throughout the day to ensure not a speck of dust remained.

When my teacher Mrs Moeketsi summoned me to the headmaster's office, I feared the worst. I shyly made my way through the short passage leading to the end of the office block, where his office was located. I stood momentarily by the wide-open door, composing myself, and then knocked. The head, Mr Tsatsi, raised his head and asked me to sit. Before I could get comfortable, Mrs Moeketsi walked through the door and sat beside me. They wasted no time congratulating me as though they could sense my nerves.

'Johannes, you are the new bell boy,' they said.

I was to be responsible for sounding the start and end of the school days and each lesson. It was a position I would hold from grade six until the end of my final year at primary, grade seven when I was thirteen.

I cannot recall who spoke first as I sat there, stunned. I was overwhelmed by a feeling of terror. This was the worst news I could have received. I felt the earth fall from under me, and I'm sure I went deaf for a moment because the next thing I knew, they were calling my name.

'Johannes?'

'I don't know. I don't think I am suitable,' I said with a shaky voice.

They both looked at me, more in amazement than disappointment.

Then Mrs Moeketsi finally asked: 'Not suitable?'

I looked away and fidgeted with my hands.

'Johannes, this is not about suitability. This is a great honour bestowed upon you. Not every student gets to be selected to ring the school bell,' Mr Tsatsi said incredulously.

Then I felt his tone change.

'Don't you dare come here and tell us you are above this position. You will ring the bell, and that is the end of that,' he declared.

My predicament was that being a bell boy meant being the school's timekeeper. It was a responsibility that included directing class changes, lunch breaks, assembly in the morning and the end of the school day. It was a hugely prominent role that would mean being in the full gaze of the entire school. Becoming the bell boy meant I would be pulled from the shadows and thrust into the bullies' spotlight. To make matters worse, I was told I would be trained by the current bell boy, who was the closest thing the school had to a rock star. Boys wanted to be like him. Girls – and even some of us boys – wanted to be with him. Why? At the end of the day, he would ring the bell with barely concealed delight. On Fridays, he would bring the school to a standstill with his bell ringing. This was the one day he was allowed to ring the bell as long and wildly as he wanted. He would even sample the popular tunes of the time. This was the guy I was being told I would initially be shadowing and then taking over from. A towering, hunky rugby player with dashing good looks and an entourage of hangers-on – the typical teen film heartthrob.

I was instructed to meet the existing bell boy at the head teacher's office the following week for training. I had to face my fears. On the day, I arrived before him. When he eventually turned up, he grabbed the bell and instructed me to follow him outside. He set off around the school buildings, paying me no further attention. When he was done ringing the bell, he walked back to the office and left the heavy instrument on the headmaster's desk. I had a dawning sense that this had been a pointless exercise and the existing bell boy had just used it as an opportunity to humiliate me.

We were told I would start ringing the bell under his supervision the following week and, for the whole of grade six, we would take it in turns ringing the bell.

From this moment, I knew I had to start watching my back again in public. The bullying had got better since my win at Johannesburg, but now I felt like I was firmly back at square one. The hardest thing about being targeted as a child is that you think you deserve it, which is probably why many children never report it. There was part of me that didn't join the dots that reporting these boys could lead to someone making them stop. I endured most of it and didn't even tell my mum how pervasive it was. My friends were at a loss to understand why I would have said yes to the position. Jeff and Seun said I should have argued harder not to do it.

'What are you thinking? You can't be serious? Your life is over,' they told me.

Even with their confidence, they saw that this role could never be a good thing for me. They were right. The worst bullying I experienced at school was to follow. I couldn't have anticipated how exposed being a bell boy would leave me. School life was about to become unbearable.

I had not realised just how heavy the bell was. It needed a boy with muscles, not a dance posture like mine. So it made sense that the current ringer had the job. He was one of those boys who possessed a loud, confident voice – the kind who is not necessarily renowned for his grades but is popular, nonetheless. For most of that year, I feared walking past the seniors' block to ring the bell. Some days I would be met with catcalling, whistling and name-calling. On other days, the older boys would sneak out of the class and chase me around, threatening to beat me up. It was so painful to go from revering the existing bell boy, whom everyone at school loved, to despising him. Whatever affection I had felt for him evaporated. It was ultimately his friends who gave me the worst time. He was never brave enough to join them, but he would laugh and cajole them while they tormented me.

Without any encouragement or real training, I would timidly do my best to ring the bell during the breaks. I also learned which blocks to avoid walking past. This didn't sit well with the head teacher, who called me and the senior bell boy to his room to let us know that he needed to hear the bell all the way from his office. He shouted at me and instructed me to ring it with sufficient vigour. Standing beside me with a smirk, the senior bell boy made sure I couldn't tell the head that his friends' habitual bullying had made it impossible for me to do the task properly. I couldn't tell him about the snide comments and the catcalling.

We left the office in silence. Inside, I was bursting to give him a piece of my mind and tell him I would report him, but words failed me. I did the one thing I knew how to do: I devised a plan. Instead of walking in front of the classrooms, I would walk behind them, looking out for my tormentors and making sure to run to the office to return the bell before they could catch me.

For a while, I felt like the most hated boy at the school. In reality, the only people who gave me grief were this small group. But in my head, the school's hatred towards me was justified. He was a charming heartthrob who knew how to hold a tune, and I was a camp, skinny boy who could hardly carry the heavy bell.

Even though he was approaching the end of his time at the school, my appointment felt like a demotion for the school's popular bell ringer, at least according to his fans. I understood that the increased levels of bullying were their protest against my appointment. I also understood that they were using my sexuality to justify their actions. I was an easy target. Mr Tsatsi insisted they wouldn't replace me and that I needed to come into my own. However, I was not to be spared. The bullying was relentless for the whole year until the senior ringer and his disciples graduated and left the school. As soon as I got back to my aunt's house or the recreation hall for dance training, I felt myself take my first full breath of the day. It would be over for another day.

As I was dealing with the increased bullying that came with being the bell boy, I hit a rocky patch in my relationship with my mum. It started when my neighbour Mona started to wear female clothing. For a long time, Mona had felt stifled because he couldn't be himself in our township. He had got to a point where he did not care what other people thought of him. He was so unhappy with his physicality that he had started to make that change.

The new Mona, dressed in heels and a skirt with long hair. I admired her deep courage. I had never seen her this happy and content.

To my horror, my mum called me home one day and told me I should never talk to or see Mona again. I was on the cusp of entering those inquisitive teenage years and, naturally, I wanted to engage further with my mother, but the door was not open. I was deeply hurt because I was old enough to understand that my mother feared the consequences of my friendship with Mona due to the stigma she now faced from the community. I wondered if her fear was rooted in the concern that, as a result of Mona's influence, I, too, might seek to start transitioning. Mum was uncomfortable with the situation.

I was gutted. I had always imagined my mum as extremely accepting and understanding of me. For the first time, I started to question her acceptance. My mother and I had never openly discussed my sexuality prior to this. Even when she had constantly reassured me of her love as a child, the fact that my bullying was due to my effeminate nature was tiptoed around. My mum was from a generation that did not discuss things like that. Talk of sex, even the heterosexual sort, was taboo. I understood this. What I didn't and couldn't fathom was my mum's disdain for and rejection of Mona. Her prohibition of our friendship was not a discussion, it was simply an instruction, and I had to work out that it was based on sexuality. I was hurt and angry, but also upset with myself for not standing up for a friend.

For many years, I have pondered what I would have done differently if I could redo that moment. I was still a child, but what would I have said to my mother if I had nothing to fear and nothing to lose? The answer has never changed: I should have embraced a friend. I would have defied my mum. I would not have lost a friend over them choosing to live life openly as themselves. I knew all too well the pain of being harassed for being myself. As hurt as I was, I respected my mother's wishes. I stopped talking to Mona and kept my distance.

When she was a bit older, Mona left our town for Johannesburg. She disappeared for months and, when she did return to Zamdela, she had undergone a gender reassignment procedure. She was now living life in a body she felt was always meant to be hers. She was beautiful. And though her transition set tongues wagging in our community, I was delighted to see my friend living her truth, even from a distance.

However, sadly, a couple of years later, Mona died. In her final years, she was gravely ill, and her family cared for her at home. Eventually, I built up the courage to go to her house to see her without my mum knowing. But her family refused to let me in, compounding my pain as her brothers told me she wanted to see me. Her parents refused to allow several of us to see her. Perhaps it was their way of protecting themselves from the community's judgement and prejudice or maybe it was just their way of dealing with the burden of caring for a gravely ill loved one. In my head, it was their retaliation for my rejection of Mona and how I abruptly ended our friendship. Hearing of her death, I withdrew into my shell and agonised over how our friendship had ended.

I kept thinking about how her story was, in many ways, my story too. She, too, just wanted to be free and live unhindered. Even though I'd had a bereavement experience with my granny's passing, Mona's felt like a senseless death, a loss that continued to haunt me for years. Her passing also left me with a profound sense of shame and guilt. I was plunged into turmoil about my place in society. I felt out of place at school and now had to contend with the fear that I might also be a disgrace to my family. Deep down, I feared my family's love was conditional on me not being 'that kind of gay' – the kind that could at any point decide to go 'too far'.

To this backdrop of hardship and hurdles, dancing gave me a sanctuary. After one win at another national contest in grade seven – my senior year – the school was notified of my victory. One day when I was in Mr Tsatsi's office to collect the bell, he asked me to confirm if it was true that I had won the Junior National Championships. Magauta and I had sailed through the rounds the previous weekend to take the title in our group.

Pleasantly surprised by how fast good news could travel, I smiled and nodded. He jolted from his chair and extended his hand to congratulate me. He told me the school was proud of me and my achievements on the dance floor. He said he was also aware of my previous wins and would like me to give the school a special performance that Friday after lunch.

The school would be assembled for a special assembly, and my partner Magauta and I would perform for the students and staff.

It had been a long time since I had last been asked to perform at school. I feared that dancing for the school would be the final nail in the coffin of my already dwindling street cred. This had the potential to ruin me. However, I had learned from bitter experience that arguing with teachers was futile.

That Friday, students gathered for assembly outside at the assembly point. Regular weekly announcements were made, songs were sung and prayers were said. Then, Magauta and I were called to the floor, boxed in by students on three sides and teachers at the front. Faith Evans and Puff Daddy's 'I'll Be Missing You' rumbled from the speakers. Magauta was dressed in her Cinderella pink dress and I was in a crisp white shirt, ironed to perfection by my mum, and trousers paired with shiny black shoes. I took my space and knew it was a space where no one could touch me. We gave a rapturous cha-cha-cha performance. The crowd was enchanted. There was cheering, clapping and whistling all around. My entire year group was willing me on. After seven years at primary school, I finally felt seen and valued by my peers.

On that high note, the headmaster called me over at the end of the assembly.

'Johannes. I am going to let everyone go home early today. Please, can you ring the bell?'

Still flooded with the adrenaline from dancing my heart out and the students' cheering, I grabbed the bell and walked out of his office, floating on cloud nine. I felt liberated at last. I told myself to let loose and ring the bell like never before. The smooth metal felt cool against my hand, and I was immersed in the raw power of the sound I created. I brought the school to a standstill for the first time since taking the position. It was a cathartic release of so much pent-up emotion. It left me feeling powerful and connected to my peers.

I watched as the other students danced in their own unique ways towards the gate to head home, sending up plumes of dust in their wake. From that moment, something inside me changed.

A shift had taken place. I claimed my spot as the bell boy who brought his magic to the role. On Fridays, I would continue to ring the bell to my heart's content. This thing that I dreaded and that I did not want before was now something that brought me so much joy and a feeling of liberation. Before I left Tsatsi Primary that year, I was awarded a certificate of appreciation for my service.

Chapter Five

Anchored . . .

Latin and ballroom dance competitions took up most of my weekends. As my successes continued to grow, I was approached by several studios with a view to joining them, but because of financial constraints, this was not always feasible. This all changed when Elvis and Patricia Paleman approached my trainer Abuti Ben, to ask that I join them. The husband and wife team, whom I knew as Uncle Elvis and Aunt Patricia, were unyielding in their quest to have me join their studio. They had a brilliant girl they felt would be a perfect match for me. Thami Tsamai and I were not only height-compatible, we were also considered to be among some of the strongest dancers in our division. Although Magauta and I were striking gold on the dance floor, she had grown much taller than me over the years, while I seemed to be lagging behind. As an art form that celebrates visual appeal and symmetry, dancers of a similar height can move more naturally, creating a balanced and harmonious look on the dance floor. It also allows dancers to make smoother transitions between steps. There were always fewer boys than girls, and talented girls were always on the lookout for new and up-and-coming talent.

Thami and I were already on friendly terms, having run into one another at dance competitions, so I knew of her talent, and it turned out that she had been scrutinising me from a distance too. It was Thami who had pleaded with her trainers, the Palemans, to poach me so that I could be paired with her at their studio. She was convinced that we had a strong chance of winning the nationals with me as her partner. Abuti Ben initially rejected the invitation as it didn't make sense on many levels. Firstly, the school, Tropicana Dance World, was far from Zamdela. Secondly, it was in a different province, Gauteng. Joining a studio that far away would have travel, cost and time implications that could hamper my progress at school.

Abuti Ben understood that my family were only happy to allow me to dance if it didn't interfere with school. After negotiations between the Palemans and Abuti Ben, the Palemans made a final bid. They were adamant that they had the necessary resources to push me to the next level. They believed that, with Thami as my partner, we would be unstoppable in the South African junior division. As their final act of persuasion, they even offered to put me up in their home. They proposed that I move to Ennerdale, a full hour away from Zamdela, to live with them and attend school near their home. Realising that they would not take no for an answer, Abuti Ben decided that they should speak to my mother and let her make the final call.

Clearly on a mission, Uncle Elvis and Aunt Patricia came to my Aunt Martha's house to make their case to her and my mother. They cheerily introduced themselves, with Aunt Patricia explaining that their school took in underprivileged children at various levels to train them to reach new heights. She told my mum that their school was special because it scouted for talent from everywhere – across the whole country. They had identified me as a dancer with natural talent and great potential, which they wanted to develop further to give me access to a bright future. They offered to take me into their care while I trained with one of their best dancers, a partner they believed was perfect for my development. Patricia explained that I had more opportunities in the Johannesburg region, as it was better resourced and funded than the Free State, where I currently trained and competed.

As Abuti Ben had foreseen, my mum said no. Not her child. I was thirteen going on fourteen and had just moved to high school, a sensitive time when some teenagers go off the rails. So letting me move away to live with another family she didn't know was not part of her plan. It also jarred with her parenting style, which was watching me like a hawk.

Realising Uncle Elvis and Aunt Patricia's sincerity, my aunt stepped in and tried to mediate.

'So what are your plans for Johannes?' she asked my mum bluntly. The room fell silent. I was relieved because I knew that if anyone could get through to Mum, it was Aunt Martha.

'Do you want Zamdela to be the end of the road for him?' she asked firmly. 'He loves to dance. He has shown how hard he works and how talented he is. This offer is a credit to that. Can't you see that? It is an invitation to the next level. The family should not stand in the way of his growth.'

Mum and I were left to speak privately.

Instead of asking me what I wanted, Mum barked, 'Are you responsible for this? Why have you put me in this position?'

I refuted the ambush and clarified that I had not orchestrated the Palemans' visit.

'But Mummy, I want to go. It is a chance I might not get again.'

Mum was genuinely taken aback by this. Of course, no parent imagines their son will leave the nest at the tender age of thirteen.

'But I can't afford to send you. I have no job. Who will pay for you?'

More potently, I knew her pride wouldn't allow her to out-source my upbringing to complete strangers. She painstakingly explained that, when I was home at Aunt Martha's, she had some peace of mind. I reminded my mother that the visitors from Ennerdale had said we would not need to worry about anything.

'They have said they will look after me,' I implored. 'They will pay for my food and clothing.'

Though not fully persuaded or perhaps feeling cornered, my mother finally relented.

I was excited beyond measure. Leaving Zamdela and getting out there to further my dance career felt liberating but bitter-sweet. I knew the opportunity would not come around again. It was a selfish decision because I knew that, as well as my family, who were sad to see me leave, Magauta and my coaches were also very upset.

Shortly after that gathering, which was to transform my life forever, a trip was arranged for us to go and meet my new partner and have a trial dance session. My mother and Aunt Martha came along for the day, and we were dropped off at the recreation centre where they trained. I didn't see much of the area that day as we went straight to the studio for the trial with Thami, followed by a short trip to the Paleman household so Mum could see where I would be living. Thami and I hit it off straight away. Shortly after, it was agreed that I would move in with the Palemans.

On the day I left home, I was accompanied by a guy called Tiro, who was asked to take me to the Palemans' home. We caught a minibus taxi from Zamdela to Vereeniging and, from there, we hopped on to a train to Ennerdale. The whole trip took about two hours.

The Palemans were from South Africa's 'coloured' community. The coloured community describes a mix of African, European and Asian populations, and this was the term used during Apartheid by the government at the time to categorise individuals who were not strictly white or black. They lived across different cities and townships, and I knew where they lived was considered a better and more multicultural area.

Because it took time to get Mum and Abuti Ben on board with the plan, I had to leave school in February that year – a month into the new school year. My new school, Fred Norman High School, was a stone's throw from the Palemans' house in Ennerdale, a town not far from Soweto. The name of the school, Fred Norman High, led me to believe this would be a 'model C' school (state-owned schools initially reserved for white children but that were now forced to open their doors to non-white children). For years, such schools were considered superior to township schools, being far better resourced.

I arrived at the Palemans' home on a Saturday to give me time to settle in before school started on the Monday. I was told to join Aunt Patricia and Uncle Elvis at the recreation centre, where I met many other dancers who were all seeking to further their craft like me. I discovered that Patricia and Elvis' home was full of young people from across the region at the weekend. Training took place at one of two nearby recreation centres.

Uncle Elvis worked as a caretaker at the municipal recreation centres, allowing us access for extended periods. On weekends, dancers often left the studio after hours and headed straight to the Palemans' for the night because public transport had already shut down. They would only venture home on Sunday evenings for school the following day.

This would be my life for the next four years. From sharing a room with my mother and sister at Aunt Martha's home, I was now sharing a room with the Palemans' son, Angelo, during the week and over twenty boys on weekends. It was a small house with a lounge, three bedrooms, a small kitchen and a single bathroom. On the weekends when everyone stayed, there would be bodies draped everywhere. If you could find a patch of floor or corner of a sofa, you would pitch up there. In the years I lived with the Palemans, a lack of privacy was the price I paid – a small price for all the beautiful moments, lessons and new experiences living there opened up for me. There was so much laughter and tears, trials and triumphs, and my coming of age, all during those four years.

When Monday came, I went to Fred Norman High and was confronted with the reality that it was not the multiracial melting pot I had anticipated. Nine out of ten students were from the 'coloured' community, and the rest were Black. This was just the first surprise. Moments after crossing the threshold into the school, I was in the headmaster's office witnessing a showdown between Aunt Patricia and the head, Principal Davy.

Despite their efforts to get me to move to Ennerdale, I had not been formally enrolled at the school. That was, at least according to the school's records. But the school soon learned that if Aunt Patricia says it's in *her* records, they had better update their own. What Aunt Patricia says goes.

The head explained that it was too late in the year to accept any students as the academic year had begun in January, and it was now the middle of February. The school roll was full and there was no room for more students.

Finally, the head revealed that the school had a policy against accepting transfer students who had not previously been taught in Afrikaans. After a long speech, Aunt Patricia looked Principal Davy in the eye and asked where he suggested I should go.

He said I should remain in my current school or try another school in extension nine, on the other side of Ennerdale.

Patricia, whose home was in extension three, said I would go to a school in extension nine over her dead body.

'Patricia, there is no space,' Mr Davy insisted.

'Mr Davy, you will make space,' she retorted, not backing off an inch.

'Patricia, you know we cannot do that,' the principal pleaded.

'Mr Davy, you know I live down the road. Why must my child go all the way to another zone? My child is coming to school here,' she said defiantly.

I stood there, watching the ping-pong exchange. Then, finally, after what felt like an eternity, Mr Davy relented and sent us to the registration office, a small room next to his office. It was the first time I had heard a woman other than my mother call me her child. I knew straight away that I would be loved and taken care of.

I was registered and taken to my new class that same day. A sense of awe overcame me as I realised that, had it not been for this spirited woman's fight, I would have had no chance of being accepted. It was also the first time I was formally introduced to the real Aunt Patricia. Perhaps I should have guessed this would be her natural approach after seeing her in action the day they came to convince my mum to let me move. This was a woman with serious negotiating skills.

Getting enrolled at Fred Norman High was the first battle of many. As I navigated life at the new school, I wish some of her 'never take no for an answer' spirit had rubbed off on me. Aunt Patricia had managed to get me through the door, but she couldn't hold my hand on the other side.

Fred Norman High was like setting foot on another planet. Lessons were conducted in Afrikaans and, having been taught in Sesotho for most of my school years, I found myself having to learn in an entirely alien language.

Not only did I not speak the language, but I was joining my class a month after the academic year had already begun. I was coming in at grade nine when my classmates had started bonding and forming cliques a full year earlier. It was like being the new kid all over again.

At my previous school, I had excellent marks. But my marks plummeted dismally from day one. I felt displaced. I was immediately struck by how the students interacted with their teachers. It was far more liberated and interactive. Before then, I had gone to schools where teachers taught and learners learned unquestioningly.

At Fred Norman High, the teacher–student dynamic was completely different. I witnessed students talking freely in class, sharing their ideas and challenging teachers. At first, I found the approach disrespectful. But over time, I learned to appreciate how it empowered students to think freely and apply themselves critically with the teachers, each other and the curriculum itself.

It was abrasive at times, particularly in how the students interacted. I had never seen so much confrontation. Then, in week one at Fred Norman High, I witnessed my first classroom brawl, which played out like a scene from the US jailhouse drama *Orange Is the New Black*. On that day, some girls had fallen out over something someone had said. After all these years, I still vividly recall the sharp sounds of tables screeching against the floor and chairs being thrown against the wall. Students screamed and cheered as a group of girls wrestled each other to the ground. I was the first to scream in horror. Not because I was being dramatic but because I was genuinely shocked.

I always kept my ear to the ground and I made my first friend in my class – a girl called Londekile Ntsiba – when I warned her that I had overheard some of her peers talk about 'jumping her'. I told her not to come back to class as they were coming for her and that, after the fight I had witnessed that week, I would get out of there. She was not in class for the rest of the day and subsequently thanked me for my help, asking to sit with me during break time.

My friendship with Londekile continued throughout high school and, later, she became my unpaid tutor.

'I don't hang out with dumb friends. I don't make friends with people who fail,' she would say constantly.

If my marks dropped, she would give me a disapproving look and we would make time to review the work together. She was from the Zulu community and, like me, Afrikaans was not her first language – but she was sharp enough to grasp the material.

Reflecting on my four years at Fred Norman High, I realise now that the first week was to prepare me for the rest of my time there. As I had joined mid-way through the school year this meant I had to learn the ropes on my own. I wasn't given a mentor to talk me through the do's and don'ts. I was on my own from the very start.

During the first week, I headed to the loo, as I'd done uneventfully before, but this time found a group of boys skipping class and smoking. They went silent as I walked through the door, making me feel uneasy. They blocked the doors of the smoke-filled cubicles, marking their territory. It was clear they would not move to let me use the facilities. Realising it was too late to retreat, I reasoned that if I was silent and didn't bother them, I might make it out alive.

I said 'hi' and walked to the urinals. As I was finishing my business, I felt a splatter of water on my back.

As I turned around, I saw the ringleader standing behind me.

'What are you doing?' I said softly at first, more inside my mouth than to anyone in particular.

'What are you doing?' I repeated, more forcefully now.

'Hey moffie,' he sneered, calling me a gay man. 'You're nobody. You are nothing, you piece of s***.'

I was dumbfounded, a deer caught in headlights. I turned around and continued zipping up my trousers.

'What the f*** are you going to do?' he asked cheekily.

I told myself to ignore him. Then the pestering started. The friends joined in, speaking Afrikaans, while others in the bathroom laughed.

He was determined to get me to retaliate, repeatedly asking what I was going to do and if I had anything to say.

Mum had taught me that the best way to deal with bullies when I was surrounded was not to respond. So I kept my head down and my mouth shut. I continued making my way towards the door.

Before I knew it, he kicked me to the ground and I was on the grimy toilet floor.

Once I hit the floor, the whole group descended on me. All I heard was, 'What did you say?', which was confounding as I had not said a word to those bastards.

I was dragged to one of the cubicles and dunked into a filthy toilet bowl that, mercifully, was not s***-filled but was full of urine.

When they were done, they left the toilet, chatting and laughing like nothing had happened.

I walked out of the toilet, gripped with shame and anger. It was my first week, and I felt I couldn't afford to make things worse for myself by reporting them. I knew I risked provoking them further. I didn't realise how dangerous this clutch of idiots was. I didn't need that. Thankfully, a girl called Yolanda saw what happened. She approached me as I stepped out of the loo and urged me to go to the office to report my attackers. I asked her to locate Angelo, Patricia's son, and give him my bags to take home. Then, without hesitation, I walked straight to the school's gate. I asked the guard to open it and, to my disbelief, he didn't protest. He opened it wide and watched as I stormed off the school grounds and disappeared around the corner.

I got to Aunt Patricia's to find the woman who helped the Palemans to clean their house. She was a kind lady from Orange Farm, about twenty minutes away from Ennerdale by car, and who spoke Sesotho. We grew very fond of each other as we spoke the same language. She often complained that the Palemans failed to pay her monthly wage and speculated about who had finished off the bread that week. Most of it was harmless banter that made us both laugh uproariously. Even though the

Palemans would sometimes be late paying her, she loved that family and couldn't bring herself to leave.

Finding her at home that day brought me the comfort I didn't even know I needed. To be able to articulate myself in my mother tongue was hugely consoling. She told me it was okay and that the worst was behind me now.

'This will pass,' she said.

She washed my shirt as I told her what those awful boys did to me. I explained why I couldn't report them, and she did not once judge me or seek to force me to do anything. When I had showered, I took a nap, woke up and went to dance practice that afternoon as if nothing had happened. I didn't tell a soul apart from her. I kept having the same conversation with myself: 'What is wrong with me? Why do people think it's okay to pick on me?'

As luck would have it, the ringleader was expelled a couple of weeks later, but not because of me. It was clear to see that he was a troubled individual. It was sad because he had an entourage that followed him like devotees of a cult.

One of the boys, Dylan, whom I secretly had a crush on, went on to become a friend in my final year. Much later, he sat me down and said he was sorry, revealing that he had never forgotten the incident. I forgave him, and we became great friends.

From that day, I never again used the boys' toilet. For the next four years, I would hold it until I got home or, when nature called, I would use the teachers' toilets. I would take a pile of papers from class and make it look like I was in the staffroom to run an errand for one of the teachers. I became a dab hand at studying the teachers' timetable and whereabouts to plausibly explain what I was doing in the staffroom if challenged. I was never caught except by one teacher. Thankfully, it was Mr L. – the only openly gay teacher in our school.

'I have been watching you,' he said when he rumbled my ploy.

I will never forget what he would say in class, proudly and defiantly: 'Ek is n moffie, maar fok, ek kry my geld.' *I am gay, but f***, I make my own money.*

I silently drew a great deal of strength from him. That day when he caught me, I told him I was sorry, but I could never again use the boys' loo. With compassion and understanding, he said it was fine. Without as much as another word, he affirmed that he understood my predicament.

Over the years, Mr L. became a source of support. He would tell me not to hesitate to reach out to him if I needed help. But, sadly, like Aunt Patricia, he could not be omnipresent.

Mr L. later recruited me and two others, Aubrey and Andile, to enter interschool dance competitions with him as our coach. Aubrey and Andile were part of Aunt Patricia and Uncle Elvis' dance club. The three of us were prolific title winners for the school, progressing from regionals to provincials and eventually the nationals. At least a handful of times each year, we three Black boys would be called up on stage in front of the whole school to be congratulated for winning the school's inter competitions. Aunt Patricia and Uncle Elvis supported us in representing the school. Aunt Patricia knew shrewdly that this could be leveraged to support her requests for us to miss school for our external dance work and competitions. This turned out to be a mixed blessing.

From my first day at Fred Norman High, I went from being gay to being 'straight'. It was like a natural reflex; a survival instinct had kicked in. But dancing was a dead giveaway and threatened to upend my carefully curated persona.

Unlike in Zamdela, where everyone already knew me, I was a new person in Ennerdale. No past, no reference, no history. I had already learned that being myself and living my truth came with a heavy price. This time around, I had the chance to rewrite the narrative, put on a mask and step into a character that could bring me some safety. I changed my walk, the way I spoke and toned down my hand gestures to imitate the boys. All I had to do was mimic those around me. Even though it was hard or not convincing, I knew I would still be safer as a somewhat unconvincing straight boy than an openly gay boy.

When I first arrived in Ennerdale, I was partnered with another girl, but after some time, I started dancing with Thami. I even went as far as dating her. Dating Thami made sense; we spent so much time together training and, at the heart of our relationship, we were good friends. We took on each other's bad days and good times. We willed success for one another. Sometimes they say that dancing is like a marriage, and that is right. Our connection ran deep and, by saying we were dating, it felt like it was the armour I needed. She must have wondered for the time we were together why I refused to go all the way every time we were presented with an opportunity. I would tell her how special she was and how she deserved a boy who would wait for her.

I longed for my voice to break, and it never really did. I often let out a high-pitched squeal when I was excited. People would look at Thami and me as we laughed and screeched together and were bemused.

Despite my best efforts, dancing betrayed me, and having a girlfriend in high school didn't keep the bullies at bay. In this coloured community I now called home, dancing was synony-mous with being a 'moffie' or a gay man. This wasn't just about me; all the other boys who danced were eyed with suspicion by a large part of the community.

'Jy wat? Jy dance? Jy's 'n moffie,' they would declare bluntly. *You what? You dance? You are gay.*

There was no hiding. Add to that, I was also tall with a lanky body. I had shot up to six foot two in my teens, which made it hard to blend in when I tried to disappear into the crowd.

It would take me years to tell Aunt Patricia about the bullying I endured at school. I kept minimising it, pushing it to the back of my head and finding ways to cope with it – or to avoid finding myself in the bullies' path. Eventually, I would point out a boy to Aunt Patricia and whisper that he was bullying me at school. I would get a kick out of watching her call them out. It was my gentle way of letting them know that I had reinforcement. I came to appreciate how much Aunt Patricia was willing to stand up for me.

In my mind, if I kept Aunt Patricia from coming to school, I

Dad in his teens

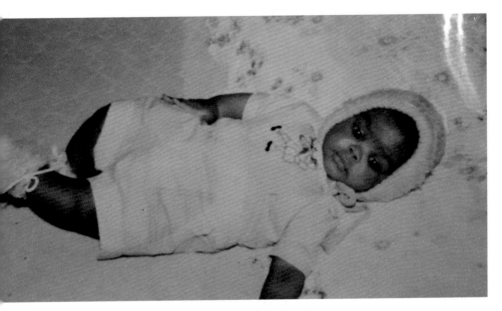

Baby Jojo

Our only picture together as a whole family

First day at Tsatsi Primary School

Reading is
fundamental, doll

My older sister,
Jabulile

Junior Pre-Championship
winners with Magauta

My first trophies

Patricia's son Angelo and Aubrey, the other boy looked after by the Palemans

Our compulsory colour-coordinated Christmas gathering

My final year
at school

Jeff and Seun,
my day ones

Me and my Aunt Martha

My Ennerdale family, Aunt Patricia and Uncle Elvis Paleman

Before, during and after: the house I built for my family

was still safe. That would be the ultimate snitch move. As a high-school student, you learn that one of the many things you leave behind is 'being a mummy's boy'. Failure to do so risks telling everyone you are weak and cannot stand up for yourself, risking open season for bullies.

Sadly, the day I had to call in my reinforcements came two years before the end of school. It was the day Malcolm, one of the bullies from my school, randomly called me a 'moffie' as I walked past him in the corridor. After two years at Fred Norman High, I had grown more confident, no longer the newbie who didn't know who was who. Most of the older bullies had either left the school or been expelled. Without thinking, I snapped.

'Jy's ook 'n moffie!' I said. *You are gay as well.*

'What did you say? After school, I am going to nail you,' he responded menacingly.

I knew that once a threat like that had been made in our school, there was no turning back. I had seen too many brawls in the classroom, on school grounds and outside the schoolyard to know this was no idle threat. What made it worse was that I had offended him in front of his peers. Not publicly defending his honour would be the height of emasculation. I was a bundle of nerves for the rest of the day. I attended most of my classes and, when the other students changed classes for the last period, I took my bag and ran.

At Fred Norman High, the school gate was locked from morn-ing until the end of school, with a guard stationed on the gate to ensure that no one escaped. It was a novelty for me as my previous schools had open-gate policies, and it was normal to quickly run home for a snack or to collect a book. Here, gates were locked up like we were imprisoned. Two years into my time at the school, I knew that leaving through the gate would not work. So when everyone turned right to go to our next class, I turned left and bolted for the hole in the fence at the back of the school, through which kids who played truant would often escape, cutting through the staffroom. Interestingly, one of our teachers, Mr Benjamin, saw me walking past the staffroom, heading to the notorious hole of 'no return'. He looked at me, and I briefly looked back at him and quietly said to myself, 'Not today, Mr Benji. Not today.'

I had resolved that I was not going to be stopped. Being dunked in the toilet was one thing, being whipped in front of the entire school would not be my story. That still happened, and kids were beaten across their hands.

I made it through the hole in the fence and ran until I got home. I found Aunt Patricia at the gate this time, chatting with someone on the street. She saw the distress on my face and stopped me in my tracks. She demanded to know what was going on. Without hesitating, I told her that it was Malcolm again. He had called me gay and, when I retorted that he was gay too, he had threatened to beat me up after school. Aunt Patricia headed towards the house. She immediately changed into neon green slippers and matching tights with a neon purple top.

'Come, let's go,' she said, emerging from the house.

'Where are we going?' I asked.

'I've had enough of this Malcolm, and today I'm going to handle this,' she said resolutely. I could see she meant business.

We marched straight to the school gate and, as we approached, the bell rang, signalling the end of the school day. I wasn't embarrassed because I was standing behind Aunt Patricia. Then, along with other kids, there came Malcolm making his way to the gate. Aunt Patricia approached him.

'Malcolm, what exactly did you say to Johannes?' she said.

Before Malcolm could clock what was happening, Aunt Patricia did the unthinkable and smacked him across the face with a loud thwack.

Once emboldened, Malcolm was now cowed. She told him that if he dared to touch or even speak to me again, he would have her to deal with. Students cleared a path for her in a way that recalled Moses parting the Red Sea as we turned to make our way back home.

It had all happened so fast, but I vividly recall the uncertainty of feeling that my life would either get significantly better or drastically worse after this moment.

Malcolm never touched me again. Every time I walked past him, I pushed my chest out, wiggled my arse and minced a little bit more. I knew he couldn't lay a finger on me. Aunt Patricia was my warrior – a woman who literally went to war for me.

Throughout my life, it has been women who have anchored me and fought for me. From my granny, who first introduced me to church and spirituality, to my mother, who protected me and taught me that her love could withstand any prejudice the world could throw me. Then my sister Jabu fought off bullies for much of my infancy. Next, Aunt Martha took us in when it became unsafe to continue living with my father. And now, there was Aunt Patricia, who fought for me to be enrolled at school and smacked bullies senseless. Despite all of my challenges, I had an army of women who blessed my childhood with comfort, love and laughter.

Chapter Six

Bound By Love

By the time I moved to Ennerdale, I had not seen Dad for what felt like an eternity. My sister and I suffered from my father's distance. It wasn't so much that Mum kept us from him, but rather that my dad's only interest in us was tied up in his insistence that we all go home to him. This was the only condition on which he would reconcile their relationship and resume his role as our father. He had set an ultimatum: they would either be a married couple living under the same roof or he would have nothing to do with us. As a child, I didn't understand the nuances of their relationship. One loves their parents despite their flaws and shortcomings, secretly wishing they will work out their differences and be a family again.

I longed to go back to the days when Dad and I would go to watch football together. It was a time that I cherished. I often thought of him and our special times together. When we were still living as a family, he invited me to join him for one of the biggest clashes of the year between his club, the Chiefs, and their arch-rivals, the Pirates. It was just as it had always been – he was a cheerful and enthusiastic fan, and I was fanatical about him.

Our reverie was cut brutally short when rival teams began brawling and people started setting fire to rubbish. The stadium, which had earlier been a place of fun and reconciliation, was transformed into the apocalypse as thousands of panicked fans were screaming, shoving, pushing and stepping on each other to escape.

In a split second, Dad was swallowed by the crowds.

'Papa!' I screamed as I scoured for him, a sea of humanity thronging the concrete stadium. There was no chance of finding a familiar face. Fans sporting identical football jerseys blended into a murky sea of bodies.

In the chaos, someone grabbed me and threw me over their shoulder as they darted towards the exit gate. I could clearly see that this man was not my father nor one of his close friends. The world was a blur as I tried to make sense of the carnage upside down on this stranger's back. I was terrified.

We eventually made it outside to a mass of fans who had been trying to get into the already-full stadium. There was simply no way of finding anyone. It was unimaginable pandemonium. Realising that finding my father in this chaos would put our lives at greater risk, the man asked me to wipe the tears from my face and promised to reunite me with my father. I was old enough to know that he was comforting me, calming me down, because there was no way to know if Dad was still alive. We got away from the mass of distraught fans outside the stadium. Still firmly in his grip, we pushed through the crowds until we were far away from the stadium. From there, he told me that we would catch a minibus taxi to his house, where we would call my family to let them know that I was safe.

Without knowing who this man was or if my father was unharmed, I nodded and clambered aboard a noisy Toyota minibus, uncertain about what would come next. In a surreal turn, it emerged that my new guardian knew my father. They were both long-standing fans of Kaizer Chiefs. After what must have seemed like an eternity for my mother, he finally reached her on the phone and told her I was safe.

The idea that my dad might have been hurt was unfathomable, and I sobbed and sobbed. Around 9pm that night, Dad walked through the door to fetch me. I cried hysterically at the sight of him, standing there, alive. I later learned that Mum had rung Dad on his mobile phone to ask if I was okay. I can only imagine the misery my father had felt having to tell the mother of his son that he didn't know where I was during those fraught hours. There is nothing more distressing for a parent than not knowing where their child is. My ever-protective mother later told my father that it would be the last time he would ever take me to a stadium. We went a couple more times after that, much to her distress.

In the middle of 2001, the year that I moved in with the Palemans, when I was fourteen, Mum asked me to visit Dad in the hospital after she'd learned that he had tuberculosis.

Thami and I had just won our section that Saturday at a dance competition in Sasolburg. After the event, I went home to Aunt Martha's for the weekend. The next day my mum and I made our way to the hospital. Our visit started badly as we could not find Dad. The nurse in charge kept reassuring us that we were in the correct ward and that he was there. Looking around, I scanned the beds again and saw familiar eyes in the distance. Dad had become so gaunt; his eyes popped out from his skull and his skin was darker. He had been a very fit guy, but the infection had eaten away at him. Growing up, I had learned from public health campaigns that tuberculosis was curable and I did not expect it could be so bad. Black men do not go to health clinics when they are unwell; they hope whatever issue they may have will go away.

Mum couldn't bear to be close to my father. I think she was in shock. Looking at him, I couldn't hold back tears. I tried to make small talk with him, to which he could not even respond. But I could see that he was trying to communicate something to me. Whenever he tried to utter a word, his breathing became ever more strained and rattling. He only had the energy to lightly squeeze my hand – speaking needed too much strength. I am still haunted that I will never know what my father wanted to tell me. However, I remember an unspoken feeling of love between us that day. I was a little boy again, dashing to football matches with him and basking in his presence.

Though drink contributed to the demise of my parents' marriage, I loved my father when he was at his best – after a few drinks when he was 'merry', but not drunk. When he was sober he could be so cold and stern, but after a few drinks he would let his inhibitions go and I got to see close-up the extent of his love. It was in those moments that he would find that sweet spot and was an incredibly affectionate person. I used to wait for when my dad was drunk to be held by him. My father was also at his most affectionate when we were at football matches. I would hear him crack jokes and release the most delightful belly laughter imaginable.

On his deathbed, I finally experienced my father both sober and affectionate. Even though he couldn't speak, my father didn't want to let go of my hand.

There's a picture of me and my dad sitting on a sofa at home, and I cherish that picture dearly – it captures our relationship perfectly. Though we are on the same piece of furniture, we are sitting at opposite ends. You can see the love in our eyes and, if you could touch it, you would feel it too. I think it is a snapshot of the complex relationship many Black men of my father's generation had with their loved ones.

After visiting hours, I returned to Ennerdale and received the news of my father's death two days later. I mourned harder than I had ever grieved for anyone; it felt like part of my heart was missing. I continued at school and dance training, and people asked how I was, but then, the next day, it would be life as normal. I buried the dream of my family ever coming together alongside my father. I carried that ache through every second of every minute, and it weighed me down. I wish that, in those times, people had asked me more if I was okay. It had been my decision to leave home, and I would beat myself up for not being there, so there was no way I would allow myself to give in to the homesickness that threatened to engulf me.

As well as the picture of me and Dad on the couch, with love in our hearts and eyes, there is one other picture that I treasure, probably more than any other. It shows my sister Jabulile and I as youngsters, flanked by Mum and Dad. I love that, in the picture, we are sitting together, side by side, as a family. In my head, I don't have any other memories of us together in one moment – as a perfect whole. By the time I started understanding the world around me, my parents' relationship had already failed. Soon after that, I would grow up and my sister would enter her teens and start doing the things that teenagers do – closing herself off from the family. As the years went by, we grew apart. But just as I was certain of my dad's affection, I have never doubted my sister's love and that she will always protect me. The picture shows a time when we were all one, and could be at one. In that lone frame, we are happy, we are together and we are bound by a love for each other that has echoed through the years.

When I left Aunt Martha's house at the age of thirteen, it never occurred to me that it would be the last time I would ever live permanently with my family. As a teen, my thoughts about the grander scheme of things were vague, clouded by adolescence. Every feeling was overwhelming and intense. Every moment felt real, deep and permanent. Caught up in the fog of my own mind, my thirteen-year-old self could not fathom that one year would turn into four, by which time I would be an adult. I would never again be home with Mum and Jabulile or with Aunt Martha and my cousins.

Living with the Palemans took time to get used to, making for one of the most interesting times of my life. At times it felt that I was starring in an American sitcom, complete with a studio audience and laughter tracks, layered with 'oohs and aahs' to highlight the drama. There was never a dull moment. Neither was there a moment of solitude. At any given moment, I was surrounded and drowned by the babble and comings and goings of other characters on the Paleman stage, each day bringing a fresh script and new plot twists. Uncle Elvis and Aunt Patricia lived with all of their four children. Angelique was the eldest, Anneline was two years older than me, while Angelo was a year younger and their only boy. Antoinette was the baby of the family. Uncle Elvis was a former tai chi champion and lived by strict discipline and structure. Aunt Patricia, on the other hand, was a mischief-maker who loved hard and fought just as hard for her loved ones. She reminded me of Aunt Martha, except that Patricia was also a prankster. The Paleman couple were complete opposites, yet they complemented each other so well.

Over the next four years, my time was mostly divided into quarters: home with the Palemans; school at Fred Norman High; competitions across the country on the weekends; and the recreation centre where we rehearsed every night and on the weekends when there were no competitions.

At the recreation centre, our weekend rehearsals would typically start at 10am and wrap up whenever Uncle Elvis decided. There were many nights when we would be there until 2am. The day would usually start with some of us who were in the championship teaching the youngsters in the morning. When we were done instructing, the intermediate and advanced dancers would then resume our own training.

Our rigorous routine was coupled with intense physical training. Uncle Elvis trained us like we were in the army, drilling us to perform 500 sit-ups and 500 push-ups on command. He worked every muscle in our bodies, strengthening our heels, legs and backs while improving our stamina. It was the most intense training I had ever experienced and cultivated an extreme work ethic and dedication that would serve me for many years to come. Uncle Elvis was not a dancer himself, but had the most incredible eye for dance and precision footwork so that we could execute sequences accurately and smoothly. The more we trained, we built muscle memory and improved technique. A lot of the choreography was self-taught and we would watch videotapes to see how the top dancers added together steps. Uncle Elvis was an anomaly in the dance world in that he demanded excellence in technique but was not creative. Instead, he would pull that out of us. When we put together a new choreography, he would critique it and tell us if it looked powerful.

When we got home after a day of training with Uncle Elvis, we would shower off the hours of sweat and sleep like logs. Being part of a large group made us push ourselves harder and intensified our drive. I found competing hard, but I always wanted to be my best and keep pushing myself harder and harder. There was a great sense of community in being part of this big club with lots of exceptional dancers.

More than eighty children made up the club, many of whom would sleep at the Palemans' house on weekends. With his modest salary, Uncle Elvis and Aunt Patricia somehow managed to keep us all fed. I genuinely believe that if they didn't have so many mouths to feed, the Palemans could have afforded themselves quite a comfortable life. On many days, I bonded with Aunt Patricia over the cooking pot, where she would attempt to make a meal for everyone. I would always help her for the sake of my other brothers and sisters. Good meals were not plentiful, but she would do her best. There were times when we couldn't eat, and I would be sent off to the shop to ask for milk on credit. Taking us all in took its toll not only on their finances, but on their family too. Uncle Elvis and Aunt Patricia didn't just stretch their income to run the club, they also divided their family time with us. During the week, we had afternoon rehearsals. On weekends, we would often rehearse until the wee hours. Their children bore the brunt of having their parents constantly away from home for hours on end. Uncle Mark, Patricia's brother, would occasionally express his disapproval of the situation, asking his sister whether he could ever walk into the house and not find it full of these 'kaffirs'.

There was a sting to his use of this word, known in polite company as 'the K-word', in full sight of all of us, but they bickered with affection and humour. That said, the word is a racist, derogatory word coined for Black, Indian and coloured people during the Apartheid era.

Without missing a beat, Aunt Patricia would retort that we were *her* 'kaffirs', and that we were in *her* house and she could do as she pleased.

She would then go on long rants, telling off Mark, scolding him for not valuing people and calling him out for using foul language in front of us.

'F*** them,' he would rail wryly. 'Why don't they go to their mother's house? We come to our sister's house, and we can't even find a seat to put our behinds down because they are scattered everywhere. Plus, you're poor yourself, but you want to feed the poor!'

These fiery exchanges could drag on until either one of them would finally walk away, or Uncle Elvis would step in to defuse the situation. It was mostly good-natured banter between siblings. Even though we all knew this, there was some truth in his jabs.

Thami and I were the only Black couple in the Youth Championships to place in the top three. Like me, Thami came from a single-parent home. The fact that both our guardians were scrambling to support us to compete in a sport that required us to have fresh and expensive costumes for each competition was hard. The Palemans, like my previous mentors Abuti Ben and Ausi Mpho, were offering us free training. When it came to costs like entry fees, transportation and costumes, it was hard for them to provide us with everything we needed. Their own children were competing too, not to mention all of us in their club. As a result, to raise funds, they would sometimes get us to dance at local shopping centres or SOS, a children's home that supported vulnerable children and their families. Thami and I would essentially get about two costumes a year that we had to reuse for various competitions against dancers who changed their costumes almost every time. I did my best to alter my costumes as I grew.

During one competition that was hosted in Gauteng, we met with one of the judges for some feedback after the results were announced. They were a dancer and judge whom I highly respected. This was our one chance to get some all-important pointers for our improvement. So, we took our shot.

'You are never going to win,' he said, his eyebrows raised slightly. 'You are simply not well-groomed enough.'

Our big grins dissolved into long faces. We were crushed; I felt my heart descend into my well-polished shoes. It was not so much that we didn't know what he had just told us, but that we had always believed that, if we worked harder, the judges would reward us. When it came to costumes, we knew we couldn't compete with dancers from affluent families, who would rock up in glamourous dresses and suits worth thousands of rands. We made do with what we had and worked hard to get our technical skills up to scratch.

To be brutally honest, it felt very much like a dividing line based on race. Most of the white kids had the best attire, and a few Black kids who came from well-off families did too. But for most of us, it was a case of pulling rabbits out of hats and making do. There were many dancers who dropped out of the competitive world because they were overwhelmed by the financial burdens and the impact inequality had on results. Sometimes I would be so angry about it and would confide in my mum when I saw her. She would tell me to never compare myself with others.

'Woah, don't compare,' she would say to me. 'Don't do that.'

I took her advice and tried not to, but sometimes it felt hard.

Thami and I were part of the A league that represented our province. This also meant we would be able to compete internationally if there was an invitation for a team to represent South

Africa, although we silently understood that going abroad would be highly unlikely due to our lack of finances. We travelled across South Africa and were always placed in our groups. However, it was hard to push on further; we did not have the right clothes or the money.

In our case, like some other community-based clubs, going to competitions took a community to accomplish it. The Palemans would regularly take more than fifty children of various ages to competitions, meaning starting as early as 3am as everyone needed to shower, iron and get their costumes ready. We'd have to leave Ennerdale at 5am to make it to an arena in time, even though the children's section would only start several hours later.

There would be days when the minibus taxi would break down, or someone would misjudge the distance we needed to travel, or a dancer was late coming from some faraway place. There would be stories of minibus taxis not being available on a competition morning and how the dancer in question would have to wait for a train when the rail service resumed at 8am. Or dancers were late because their parents were running from neighbour to distant cousin, trying to raise funds for travel on the morning of the competition. These were not lame excuses – they were the unfortunate reality of the situation. I was not the only one living by the seat of my pants.

It was against that backdrop that you would walk onto the floor and dance your heart out. For a few minutes, you escaped to a different world. You would forget all the hardships that had to be overcome to get there and the behind-the-scenes drama, all while competing with dancers who arrived just two hours before their division. They would be as fresh as daisies, backed by a cheerleading team that included their mum, dad and maybe even grandparents and siblings for moral support.

Sadly, some children would arrive only to find they had missed their sections. Parents would be devastated and their children would sob. Big trips like those to the nationals in South Africa's famed Sun City casino resort would have taken months of planning and fundraising. To make it all the way there and be told your child cannot compete because they have missed their section was a disaster.

By the time I was due to dance in my section in the competition in Gauteng, it was around 8pm and I had already been up for seventeen hours. We had spent the day helping the rest of our juniors and extinguishing the little fires that erupted throughout the day.

To know the hurdles we had cleared to make it to the dance floor in one piece, only to be told that we would never win because we were not well-groomed, was a huge slap in the face. Grooming is admittedly a big part of the Latin and ballroom tradition, and dancers are expected to be dolled up from head to toe. Presentation of your garment, hair and shoes is part of your adjudication scoreboard. We were essentially being told to get more money if we wanted to win. What the adjudicator had also neglected to tell us that day was that there was a set syllabus being privately taught to studios with wealthy members.

For children who could afford it, they had some of the top adjudicators come in to give special workshops leading up to competitions. In these workshops, the dancers would be finessed on what the judges were looking out for on the floor, giving them an advantage over dancers who could not afford such tuition. It was a tricky situation. The same people who adjudicated us often ran the workshops, and some even had their own studios where they had dancers they were personally grooming. Money was the key that unlocked the upper reaches of the dancing world.

Fortunately, Aunt Patricia understood the politics. She was a community leader who approached everyone for help. She would pool from every resource she could find. She rang up and stalked one of the top dancers in the country, Tebogo Kgobokoe, who also happened to be a well-respected adjudicator. Aunt Patricia invited Tebogo to visit our studio to offer us some valuable pointers. After months of pestering and endless calls from Aunt Patricia, Tebogo agreed to make the drive to us, giving us a free workshop. Aunt Patricia's sob story about what it would mean for us to be given equal chances as the dancers from better-off studios, must have tugged at Tebogo's heartstrings.

After we found out she was coming, my partner and I learned one of Tebogo's award-winning choreographies off by heart with help from Uncle Elvis. We had been studying her work from the time we began dancing, and she was one of the country's most revered dancers. We watched her samba on an old videotape over and over again until we perfected every bounce, sharp turn and bold razor-sharp stare for which she was so celebrated.

By the time she came to our studio, we were ready to demonstrate it to her. She was overcome with emotion. At the beginning, she thought we had plagiarised her routine, until she understood that we had actually learned it in her honour. We had copied every last detail and, while it was not the done thing, I think she eventually clocked why we had done so. Still emotional, she tied her hair into a ponytail and danced the routine with us.

At the end of the session, she offered us the routine and made alterations to make it new for us. She gave her blessing for us to compete with it. Tebogo's visit was a major turning point for me and Thami. Tebogo was South Africa's undefeated champion, and her visit reaffirmed us.

'If you love dance as much as you say you do, you must always, always – with every opportunity you are given – leave your hearts on that floor,' she said as she left. 'If that is your objective for every performance, no one can ever overlook you again.'

Living with the Palemans was a thoroughly consuming experience. Outside of the seven hours that I spent at school, most of my time was with them. In short order, I had learned how to speak Afrikaans, the language spoken in Ennerdale, and had also adjusted to all their individual traits and characters. By the end of that first year, Ennerdale felt like home and the Palemans had done their best to make me feel like I was family. We ate together, sitting around joking, gossiping and laughing until late at night, and I equally shared in the family chores.

We had a dishwashing schedule that wouldn't stick no matter how hard we tried. Many nights we would be bantering late into the evening, when Aunt Patricia would ask whose turn it was to don the marigolds that night. I would protest that I had washed the dishes the night before and that it was Angelo's turn. Angelo would nod and then continue goofing around, and then, when nobody was paying attention, he'd sneak off to bed without washing up. He always knew that I would eventually cave in and do it. When I first moved in with the family, I did this without complaint. Then, as I got more comfortable, I started asserting myself.

One night when Angelo pulled the same stunt again, Aunt Patricia decided it was time to put an end to the saga. She must have started asking whose dishwashing turn it was from about 8pm that night, and it was Angelo's. By 10pm, the dishes had still not been washed and Aunt Patricia was still asking.

'It's Angelo's turn, Mummy!' we all responded in chorus. (I always called her 'Mummy' to her face and she used my family nickname, Baba.)

'But where's Angelo?' Patricia asked.

'He's sleeping,' everyone responded.

'Angelo is tired, Patricia. He was feeding the dogs,' Elvis chipped in.

Without a word, Aunt Patricia stepped into the bathroom and, when she came back out, she was holding a bucket full of water. She headed straight to Angelo's room and tossed the whole bucket over his bed. As Angelo was rudely awoken by the ice-cold water, Patricia made her way back to the bathroom to refill the bucket. At this point, Anneline woke, picked up her blankets and walked to our neighbour's house to sleep. Angelique barricaded her door with her full frame. No bucket of water was going to land on her bed; she was ready to fight. Angelo got up and, instead of strutting to the kitchen to wash the dishes, he grabbed whatever dry sheets he could retrieve from his bed and climbed to the top of the flat roof to sleep there, out of his mother's reach. With nowhere to go, and no desire to sleep on a wet bed in the middle of winter, I resigned myself to washing the dishes to resolve the drama. Peace was restored.

Throughout the four years that I lived with her, Aunt Patricia did more than fight bullies on my behalf; she also arm-wrestled teachers on multiple occasions when my studies and my dance schedule clashed. In my last year of school, another dancer from the club, Andile Ndlovu, and I were invited to be part of one of South Africa's leading youth ballet companies of the nineties and noughties, Ballet Theatre Afrikan (BTA). Under the leadership of Martin Schönberg, BTA was to run a season at the prestigious South African State Theatre. Andile and I were both thrilled and honoured to be invited to work with the revered Schönberg. In those years, BTA was renowned for producing some of South Africa's most reputed classical dancers of colour. Martin was a pioneer who had an eye and talent for training dancers from townships like Alexandra, Tembisa and Soweto, and grooming them to international stardom.

Working with Martin was tough. Similar to Uncle Elvis, Martin ran his studio like a military base. He was a highly skilled ballet technician with some rather unconventional and, some might argue, excessive training methods. For instance, stretch and strengthening classes went on for hours, and he would spend ages focusing on a single exercise. Working with Martin for those months leading up to the show's opening gave me a taste of life in a professional dance company. Sadly, during this time, my studies took a knock. The show was intense, with a punishing rehearsal schedule, and not even the special arrangements made with the school regarding my assignments and classwork were enough to keep me from struggling academically.

The dance season went swimmingly. At the end of it, both Andile and I were invited to join the ballet company – a great honour and one which I would have been happy to accept alongside my Latin dance work with Aunt Patricia's studio. But we were told that it would either be ballet or Latin, and that we couldn't do both.

Latin American dance was my home; a world I had thrown myself into for close to a decade at that point. Here I was being offered a chance to pivot, to consider a different world all together – still dancing, but a whole new world nonetheless, one that fascinated me but didn't thrill me as much as Latin. I knew that, deep inside, I was a Latin boy. I appreciated the grace, poise and elegance of classical ballet, but the wild child in me wanted to samba and cha-cha-cha.

Andile ended up taking the offer and went on to become one of South Africa's top exports and among the finest ballet dancers in the world. He is currently based in Washington, working with The Washington Ballet. I, on the other hand, bowed out at the end of the ballet season at the State Theatre and went back to my world of ballroom and Latin. Latin was and will forever be my first love.

After the season with BTA, I returned to Fred Norman High. I had some work to catch up on after my two weeks out, including an English essay to submit. Thinking the English teacher would have forgotten that I hadn't handed it in, I returned to class with my fingers crossed. When he asked for it, I had to admit that it was not yet written.

Mr Clarins told me unequivocally that I needn't bother submitting it and that I might as well grab my bags and go home because the only future I had was as the world's greatest dancer. His sarcasm in front of the whole class was stinging. It was made worse by the fact that all my teachers had been informed that I would be missing school for the two weeks that I was away working with BTA. My other teacher, Mrs Mosavel, also ridiculed me during class. She said that other students managed to dance and still hand in their schoolwork and that she was unconcerned as she was not the one who needed to pass the year.

This was hard to bear, but in all honesty, I couldn't blame them. It is hard to balance professional work and school, particularly at such a young age. I also believe that, had my teachers not expressed their disappointment with me, I probably would not have pushed myself as hard as I needed to get through school.

What I didn't see coming was the school's decision to exclude me as a candidate registered at their school. Fred Norman High wanted to achieve a 100 per cent pass rate for their final-year class. This was a big deal for many schools as, in South Africa, so-called 'matric' (A-Level) results are shared in national news-papers, and high-performing schools are publicly celebrated. Shortly before my final exams, I received my examination num-ber and discovered that I had been enrolled as a private candi-date, meaning I had been deregistered as a student of Fred Norman High, something for which I was not forewarned. The school felt that the weeks of classes which I had missed due to the rehearsals and show with BTA had put me at risk of failing the year. They couldn't compromise the school's standing and 100 per cent pass rate for one student. The teachers and head-master had decided among themselves that this was the best way forward. Overcome with emotion, I got home in tears. I had stomached the teachers' snide comments and sarcasm for days. This was the final straw. In those days, homeschooling was still very much frowned upon. Where you went to school mattered as much as your grades.

'Over my dead body,' said Aunt Patricia characteristically. 'Give me my flip-flops. Let's go.'

We arrived at Mr Davy's office, brandishing the enrolment notice and demanding to know what was going on.

'No, Patricia, we want a 100 per cent pass rate. Johannes has been dancing, and it's good for him. But we have decided this is the way to go,' he said.

'I will burn this school. I will burn this whole school down before you can deregister my child without our consent,' she thundered.

Unsurprisingly, by the time we walked out of the office, the Department of Education had been called, and I was back on the school's list of candidates.

The pressure to pass my final exams was now on, especially as so many of my teachers apparently didn't think I could. I knew, though, that it was not because they deemed me academically abysmal. Over the years, my teachers had always affirmed that I could be brilliant, but I didn't have time for my books. I needed to get my head down, and, for a short while, I turned my laser-sharp focus, which was normally reserved for dance training, to revising for my exams.

The end of the year came, and I passed. I was relieved that my hard work had paid off. Yet more than that, I felt proud. Yet again, I felt that I had proven that I was good enough. I was one step closer to joining Aunt Martha as the second member of my family to make it to university. Sadly, along with wrapping up that year at school, my time with the Palemans was also drawing to an end.

The last South African championships that year were hosted in Free State province. Together with Uncle Elvis, my partner Thami and another couple, Sizwe and Rosie, we embarked on the seven-hour train ride from Johannesburg to Bloemfontein. That competition weekend, we won our section, and I got to even spend time with my coaches from Zamdela and share a rented apartment with some of the dancers from home. We very easily fell into step with our shared histories and passion for movement.

Sitting on the train on the way back, the events of the past four years hit me all at once, overwhelming me. Much like most of my childhood, my time in Ennerdale can be best described as complicated. On the one hand, there was the love, laughter and security of living with the Palemans; on the other, there was the horrid backdrop of being bullied and chased around with a baseball bat because I was different.

The train from Bloemfontein to Ennerdale passes Sasolburg, the closest town to Zamdela, and, as it approached the stop, I stood up, reached for my backpack and bid farewell to the group.

'Uncle Elvis, thank you for everything. Thami, I love you partner. Sizwe and Rosie, all the best,' I said. 'Send my regards to everyone when you get back home.'

At this point, I don't think any of us thought this would be the end. Perhaps even I thought I would return the following year after the festive season. All I knew was that I was relieved that school was finally over. The excitement of what my life could become was starting to sweep over me. In a twisted way, it felt like I was being released from prison. I wanted to go home. I didn't know what lay ahead; I just knew that I now had the freedom to live more freely. It felt liberating.

Chapter Seven

I'm Here

When I stepped off the train in Sasolburg that day, I was a different person from the thirteen-year-old who had left to pursue my dream to dance four years earlier. I was a young man ready to face a new chapter. And yet here I was, returning to the nest, running back to my mother's embrace as I drafted the next part of my story.

When my final-year results came out, I had to seriously and quickly consider where I would be going to start university the following month. Unlike more astute students who had already applied during their twelfth grade, I hadn't and so had to wait for my results to come out. It had always been hammered into me that education was my only pathway to a better life – the one key that could positively unlock my future. I knew that going to university was a non-negotiable for me. The understanding that I would continue my studies after high school was undoubtedly the only reason my family had allowed me to dance. Dance was never going to be something that allowed me to live; I would need to have a profession in the future in order to survive. There was no other way.

With the help of Aunt Martha, we managed to get together enough money for me to register for a Public Relations degree at the Vaal University of Technology. All other courses were full, but I ploughed on nonetheless. In my eagerness, I ignored many financial red flags fluttering before me. For starters, my mum didn't work. Secondly, my father had died, which meant he could not help. And Aunt Martha, despite her willingness, had to put the needs of her own children first. I could not afford higher education.

After six months of trying to push through my first year on a shoestring, reality hit and I had to drop out. It was painfully clear that continuing to study was not financially viable. During the six months that I was enrolled, I joined the university's dance club and, fortunately, I was able to continue even when I dropped out of my studies. I literally danced my way through those six months and did some teaching. It was the only way to stay around. Every year there was a dance competition between universities called the SASSU Tournament. I used to choreograph dance team formations, and we would always win.

The following year, I reapplied for the academic programme, going instead for something much closer to my heart than PR – interior design and decor. I hoped that the small allowance that I was getting from the university for tournaments and the choreography work that I did for the college would help me cover my tuition. In reality, the money was so little that it only helped me to eat. Learning on an empty stomach was a reality I had come to understand. I never starved while going to school, but I didn't always have enough. Sharing limited resources with fifty others at the Palemans' had taught me to make do.

At university, I lived off tins of baked beans and bread for weeks. Nonetheless, I thrived during my second year. I loved my coursework and, as my finances became ever more precarious, I fought hard to stay in school. It was about halfway through the year when I was cast in a stage production of *Takalani Sesame*, a popular South African kids' TV show. The Rand Easter Show was back for its annual Easter week at a vast showground outside of Johannesburg. Every year, droves of families would descend on the venue for stage shows, rides and shopping stalls. *Takalani* was putting on a stage adaptation of its show on the main stage. I was cast as Moses and offered 12,000 rands for twelve days' work. It was the highest-paying gig I had ever had.

'Johannes, 12,000 rands for twelve days of work is more than what I make as a professor,' said my lecturer at the time. 'Look, your studies are going to suffer. Twelve days is two weeks' worth of lectures. As it is, you are hardly ever in class because you are hustling. You are academically strong, but attendance is key for you to sit the exams. I don't know what to tell you, but if I was in your position, I'd probably make this dance thing work.'

It was hard for me to walk away from the university. I understood that the university had a strict attendance policy. I also recognised that 12,000 rands could not only make a difference in my own life, but it would also allow me to help Mum. I called her.

'Listen, Mummy. I am hungry, and I have been offered a job. I wonder how you are holding up your end? I have spoken to my teacher, and she has advised me.'

'What has she advised you?'

'That I need to take the job. I can always come back to school and study. But I need to take this money.'

Three years after my father's passing, my sister was pregnant, and my aunt was not comfortable with having three mothers under one roof. Dad didn't have siblings, so my mum inherited the family home. As Jabulile prepared to give birth, my mother, who was still my father's legal wife, was given the chance to move into her old home after spending a decade with her sister. For years, the house had stood empty, and it had become derelict. The warmth and love with which Mum had imbued the house was long gone. It was now dark and devoid of attention. All of this was happening as I was starting university. When Jabulile and her newly born baby, my adorable nephew Rethabile, had settled in with Mum, I realised someone would have to ensure the family was provided for. Around this time, Mum started work as a caretaker at a fuel station. It was a job that didn't pay her much, but afforded her some independence. A year later, Jabulile gave birth to my niece, the lovely Bokamoso – her second child in two years.

Recognising that it was my moment to step up as a provider, I called Tebogo Kgobokoe to inquire about possible work once the Easter show wrapped. She offered me a teaching job with her studio in Bryanston, an upmarket suburb of Johannesburg. I was nineteen years old and was holding down my first full-time job. After my double exit from university, I was feeling the pressure of being the provider at home. I had taken out a loan to cover my expenses. I knew I would have to repay it sometime, so I just kicked the can down the road.

Before I started teaching, Ausi Tebogo had warned me to buy a crisp white shirt, so people took me seriously and so I looked the part. I had followed this advice, and it worked. I looked right, and that was part of my training.

I soon discovered that teaching doesn't pay much. I supplemented my salary by doing gigs here and there. Auditions are relatively plentiful in South Africa, but are also highly competitive. All my work at that stage was in Johannesburg – it's where all the major studios, choreographers, theatres, TV production companies and shows are based. Unfortunately, I was not making enough money to afford an apartment in Johannesburg – or anywhere close. For a while, I travelled between Johannesburg and Sasolburg while teaching at the studio. I would take buses and taxis, and it took around three hours each way. It was relentless and very expensive.

When the costs started getting too much, I began sneaking into the studio to sleep after we had closed for the day. We had a small staffroom where there were blankets for when we were cold during the winter months. I would put them on the floor and settle down for the night. I slept badly, but I no longer had to get up at dawn to make my first class of the day.

The studio offered social dancing evenings and, on those days, the studio would close late, so I couldn't stay there. On those nights, I would arrive at the notorious Noord minibus taxi rank in the heart of Johannesburg city centre just after the last service to Zamdela had departed. I would have to pay the drivers to sleep in the back of their vehicles for the night. Many of them swore at me and told me to get lost, but I kept trying until one would ask me how much money I had. I became friendly with a few of them and, for 10 rands or whatever I had, they would let me climb into the back seat. I knew it was dangerous, but I had no choice. I always hoped I would see a face I knew and that they were not at the other end of Johannesburg when I needed to rest. The next morning, I would wake up, wash in the filthy basins at the taxi rank and head back to Bryanston to do it all over again. This was the only way I could make ends meet.

For close to a year, I slept at the dance studio or in taxis without Tebogo's knowledge. There were days when she would work late or request the keys because they would be coming in first thing the next morning for an early private class. On those days, I would pretend to leave, then hide behind Pick n Pay, a supermarket that was adjacent to our studio. Having left the bathroom window open, I would sneak right back into the studio the minute the lights went off. I would sleep there and wake up bright and early the next morning to shower and wait outside. A few minutes after Tebogo would come in, I would follow her as though I had just arrived.

There were times when my new friend at the time, Carl, would invite me to stay over at his place. He worked as a junior accountant, but a love for dance was our common interest, a shared passion that gave way to a beautiful friendship which blossomed between us. On the weekends when he was available, Carl would pick me up, we would party the night away and he would invite me to sleep at his house. Carl was one of the few people who I trusted with the truth about my secret sleeping arrangement.

Carl and I explored the clubs of Braamfontein in Johannesburg city centre, as well as Melville, home to queer clubs like Liquid Blue. It was in those spaces that I became acutely aware of the attention that I was drawing from mostly older gentlemen.

Knowing that they had an interest in me, as some offered drinks, lifts and pleasant conversation, I saw an opportunity to see if they could assist with my lodging dilemma. I knew there were older white men keeping Black boys. I was fully aware that this happened, but the idea of asking for money or financial support from them did not cross my mind. All I wanted was to know if they had an extra room in their house or a backyard cottage, commonly known as maid quarters in South Africa, which I could sublet at an affordable price while I found my feet. Many of these men were kind enough to let me sleep in their spare rooms when I was stranded for the night. To distract them from any salacious expectations they might have had, I played immature and asked them for time before we rushed into anything. Because of my age, it worked. They understood that, at nineteen, it was normal to still be in your shell and trying to figure out your place in the world.

However, on one occasion, a man invited me for a sleepover after noticing that I was stranded. At first, he appeared sympathetic to my situation: a young dancer from Zamdela, working until late, out for a drink after a long night, needing somewhere to crash. In my desperation to have somewhere to sleep that night, I had allowed him to believe a romantic relationship could possibly develop. I had resorted to that for survival. In my mind, giving someone 'a little hope' didn't mean transactional sex. This was a mistake. The man who had promised me a spare room for the night led me to his car and drove us to his house. When we arrived there, he offered me alcohol which I politely declined, saying I didn't drink as I was a clean-living athlete. He became aggressive and insisted that I have a glass of wine. I was startled and, realising that I had lost my composure, I decided to accept, telling myself that one glass would not hurt. Slowly sipping from the glass, I became alarmed by his increasingly pushy advances. He reached over and started grabbing me, pulling me towards him. I politely told him that this was not going to work, but the more I said, 'No please, stop, relax, take it easy', the more the situation escalated.

I turned to look at the door and noticed that it was not closed. This was only one hurdle cleared. Upscale properties in Johannesburg are almost all nestled behind walls so high that they hide whatever happens behind them. After carefully considering the door, the wall that I would most likely have to climb and the pit bull barking outside, I slipped out of his grip and made a run for the door. Without even picking up my phone or bag, I jumped the wall and ran through the streets of Rivonia suburb, in the north of Johannesburg, not knowing where I was headed. What I did know was that something wasn't right, and I needed to get out immediately. I don't know what would have happened if that man had had his way. To this day, I cannot explain how I vaulted the wall, which was about six-foot high.

I walked around in circles until sunrise. My fear was that the man would come searching for me. I thought about heading to the police station, but felt that they might not believe me. I was embarrassed and, in my panic, I blamed myself for the situation. When the sun finally rose after what felt like a truly dark night, I managed to call Carl from a payphone and headed home.

Safely back at my mother's house, I vowed never to be in a situation like that again. I'd had enough – it was all too much. Sleeping in minibus taxis, on studio floors and gambling on the kindness of older men for a place to sleep was not a safe way for anyone to live. I questioned whether any of it was even worth it. Without formally resigning from my position at the studio and without any communication, I did not show up for work the following Monday and just ignored Tebogo's calls for days.

Eventually, Mum came to my room and told me to return Tebogo's calls.

'That woman has been calling you for days. Answer her and explain what happened,' she snarled.

I had not told Mum the full story. I had only told her that working for the studio had put me in a situation where I felt unsafe.

'Whatever you are not telling me, get up and go face her and tell her,' she urged.

The next day, I went back to the studio and had a heart-to-heart with Ausi Tebogo. I shared the difficulties of working in the studio while living so far away on such a modest income. She understood and apologised for not having helped more. She took immediate action. For a start, she said that I could sleep in the studio whenever I needed to. It was not the same as getting a place of my own, but at least I didn't have to live with the guilt of sneaking around. This continued for a while.

As well as Ausi Tebogo's support, the dance students themselves showered me with love and care. My students consisted mostly of ordinary people of all ethnicities, ages and abilities who wanted to dance socially for fun. Over time, we grew so close that some of them became real friends, mentors and cheerleaders. I started to see some of them as more than my students because they would always offload on to me, telling me about their latest work or personal dilemmas. I found things in common with every one of them, despite our different situations, and that was a beautiful thing. The older ones especially would jokingly complain and say I didn't teach them because we were chatting so much. We talked about everything under the sun.

During one of our Friday social dancing nights, one of South Africa's top professional dancers, Muntu Ngubane, a performer I grew up watching and admiring, came to visit. Not only was Muntu someone I admired, but he had also become an older brother in the dance world. There were times when I was competing and then auditioning, that he would host me at his house when I needed somewhere to stay. During one of my breaks from working the room dancing with various ladies in the studio, he called me aside to ask me to consider auditioning for cruise ships. He said that, with my height and talent, I would be a good fit for them. When he told me there were auditions that Sunday, I still wasn't convinced he was talking to the right person.

With all the confidence I had in my dancing, I had not thought that much about my prospects. I didn't grow up in a world where I was exposed to much, and my environment led me to believe that I could only go so far. I didn't have that unshakeable belief in my talent. I never felt it would be enough to be anything other than a champion. Even with all the affirmation I got from my backers like Abuti Ben and Aunt Martha, my family background made me believe there was a limit to how far I could go. I was jaded by the politics of the dance world, lacked self-belief and, frankly, didn't think I deserved much. Muntu knew about my financial challenges. This was his way of advising me to look beyond just being a teacher as well as to broaden my horizons beyond South Africa. But mentally, I had not made the leap to consider this as a possible way of making money. None of the people I had seen growing up had made money from dancing. Even the best of the best kept dancing as something they did for love.

In passing, I told one of the students, Jane Fry, about the audition. Jane was a good friend and also one of my favourite students because she loved to dance. She was one of the only people who used to come in and say, 'Please don't talk to me. Let's dance.'

She came to me twice a week, and I knew a lot about her life, working as a financier for films. I had also been to dinner at her lovely home.

She stopped me and looked me in the eye.

'Well, you are going to go,' she said without hesitation.

'No, I'm not,' I countered. 'Why would I want to leave you guys and the studio?'

'You are going,' she said.

'Okay, if you say so,' I chuckled.

She then asked me what I needed. I told her that I needed a lot. I didn't even have trainers.

I put the conversation out of my mind and got on with the business of partying with Carl. Having done our rounds in Melville and Braamfontein, we ended up back at the studio in the early hours of Sunday morning – the day of the audition.

I was woken up by a phone call.

'Where are you?' Jane asked.

'At the studio,' I replied slightly grumpily.

'Okay, great, I am outside,' she said.

I asked her what she was doing there.

'The audition starts in two hours. Get ready and I'll meet you outside,' she said, promising to get me something to eat for breakfast.

I related the surreal situation to Carl, who jumped from the floor with joy.

We eventually made it to the car where, sitting on the front seat, was a box of trainers. I was overcome with emotion. I snapped out of my self-doubt and psyched myself up for the audition. Jane had done something truly selfless for me, and my hangover was displaced by mounting excitement and anticipation.

Already grateful for the morning's turn of events, the choreographer announcing he wanted to start with the Latin piece made me feel like luck was on my side.

The room was packed with industry names. There were clearly dancers who had worked with the choreographer before, and the pressure was suffocating. Whenever I feel anxious, I start to feel like I can't breathe, like I have a vice around my chest. I told myself to stop and take a breath.

Carl and I looked at each other as we realised the choreographer was not particularly well-versed in Latin American technique. The samba walks were out of time. The voltas (a common samba step) went in the wrong direction.

After doing my thing, the choreographer approached me.

'Hey you, Salome Sechele,' he said.

Salome Sechele is a pioneering and iconic South African Latin and ballroom dance champion who also served as a judge on South Africa's edition of *Strictly Come Dancing*. There was laughter in the room.

'Are you a Latin dancer? I don't know why I'm even asking because your spins, my dear. Show them again,' he said.

I saw Carl beaming from ear to ear.

After the audition, the choreographer asked for my name and where I was from.

He nodded at my response, sizing me up.

'Do you have a passport?' he asked.

I didn't, but wondered if I should have told him otherwise and just sorted it out.

'No wonder, one can tell that you are from Sasolburg,' he said.

As I was despairing at his rudeness, a judge called Manalo, who was from Spain, asked me to see him after the audition.

'You are going to Italy,' Carl whispered in my ear conspiratorially.

I pushed back, reminding him that no one had yet been offered a contract. After the audition, I made my way to Mr Manalo's table.

'Hi Sir. You said that I must come and see you,' I said.

'Yes, you don't have a passport, why?' he asked with a heavy Spanish accent.

Without thinking, I responded honestly that I had never needed a passport. I had never had the money to travel, even when I'd had the opportunity. Manalo looked at me quizzically.

'You have no clue, do you?' he said to my confusion. 'Johannes, if you bag this job, we pay you a salary every month. We pay for your accommodation and transportation. You basically wake up, take a dump and dance.'

'No, that can't be true,' I said in disbelief.

'Well, go get a passport and see how true it is,' he said with a flourish. 'You are leaving a month from today.'

When I arrived home, my contract had already been sent over. Things moved at a whirlwind pace. I started rehearsals the very next week. I immediately handed in my resignation to Ausi Tebogo. She was sad to see me leave, but wished me well with my new adventure, going as far as telling me her studio would always be home if I ever needed to come back.

After I had received my contract, which Jane looked over for me, and signed on the dotted line, I told my mum that our lives were going to be better for a while. I think she would believe it when she saw it. No one in my family had ever left South Africa, so the idea of me going off to Italy and earning money through performing seemed beyond comprehension. Just as when I had left Zamdela to move in with the Palemans, I did not realise how this moment was ultimately going to change my life beyond recognition. Even I did not really believe it could be true. All I could foresee was a couple of months of earning a salary that was vastly better than the 12 grand I made as Moses.

My excitement and momentum were dashed when I had a sudden health scare. During rehearsals and while I was waiting for my passport to be delivered, I began to feel mounting discomfort which grew into unbearable pain around my testicles. Not knowing who to turn to in Johannesburg, I ran to Ausi Tebogo to share my excruciating agony. I have danced hard over the years and suffered from injuries, but this feeling was visceral and seemed to surpass the boundaries of pain. It was unbearable; I have never felt pain like it.

She took me to Life Hospital, where I was given morphine and sent home, where the pain resurfaced with such intensity that I couldn't push through. Emanating from my testicles, the pain seared through every fibre of my being. Fortunately, it was a week before our departure, so rehearsals were done. We were given a week to get our affairs together and, in that time, Tebogo took me to a private doctor who quickly determined that I needed emergency surgery.

By that stage, one of my testicles was green and blue. I couldn't pee. I had a serious infection, and the doctor referred me to Sunninghill Hospital, where I was told that a surgeon was available, but the operation would cost upwards of 80,000 rands.

Ausi Tebogo explained that we didn't have that kind of money. I was subsequently referred to Baragwanath Hospital, a public hospital, where the bill would be just 40 rands. Having spent two days running around with me, Ausi Tebogo took me to the hospital's emergency wing, paid the 40 bucks, and called my mum before leaving me at the hospital. The hospital, like many of the public hospitals, was characterised by outdated infrastructure and inadequate facilities, with overcrowding a frequent issue. I just wanted to be free from the pain.

Mum arrived at the hospital, which had no free beds nor clean blankets, late that evening with a blanket and some food. I was told to wait until a bed became available that night. The night seemed to stretch my limits of endurance. Time passed at an agonisingly slow crawl, the seconds ticking by at a snail's pace.

I went under the knife the next morning, and one of my testicles was removed. The doctor said that had I arrived one day later, I would have lost both.

South Africa's hospitals train some of the best doctors and nurses in the world. Seeing as I had only paid 40 rands, I was fair game for student training. After the operation, a bunch of students gathered around the bedside to see me, legs akimbo, while the doctor examined my lone testicle to see how the operation had gone. I could have died on the spot.

A day later, one of my friends and students, Nicolette, came to fetch me in her silver Mercedes SLK convertible. I had been offered an artificial testicle, but it would prolong the process, and I needed to get better quickly. Being picked up at this earthy public hospital in a luxury car was surreal, but she insisted that

I did not bother my mum. She would look after me. I stayed with her and her family in their beautiful home in Morningside until I was able to return for a check-up and to have my stitches removed. She had help at home, and I just lay in crisp white sheets for days while the maid fetched me food and drinks. I was served like a king.

A week after the surgery, the other successful dancers set off for their new life on the cruise ships while I waited for my medical clearance from the hospital. It was ten days until my next consultation when the stitches were due to be removed. But as they were about to be removed, it became clear the skin had not attached. The doctor looked at me and told me that I needed more time for the skin to come together. He was concerned that if anything happened to my wound on the flight, I could be at serious risk.

'Doctor, I'm going,' I said defiantly.

He warned me that I risked my ability to have kids, to which I told him I didn't need kids. I had been looked after so well at Nicolette's, and I was no longer in pain.

My Aunt Martha, who had come with me, gave me an extremely disapproving look.

'Take out the stitches, doctor. I am going to Italy,' I said over her silent disapproval.

After the doctor had taken out the stitches, Nicolette drove me to Zamdela to say goodbye to my family before I headed to the airport. It felt surreal and like another new lease of life.

This wasn't just about making it in time to start a new job, it was an escape – my chance to get away from a system that was rigged to my disadvantage. What I couldn't tell Manalo the day he had asked me about my passport, was how much the odds had been stacked against me. I couldn't tell him that after close to fifteen years of commitment and dedication, I had learned that, by virtue of being poor and Black, I stood no chance. After winning the world trials in South Africa for several years, I had been presented with opportunity after opportunity to represent my country internationally – and nothing ever came of it. I wanted to see more.

Even when a dancer was objectively at the top of their game, it would boil down to whose parents and network could afford to sponsor their child's international travel costs while representing the country. So many times, I saw dancers who were placed in the second-tier 'B league' get to represent the country because the dancers in the A league could not afford to go abroad. I wondered what message this state of affairs was sending to talented dancers from less well-off backgrounds like me. Any child told that, no matter how hard they try, they will fall short because of circumstances beyond their control will inevitably lower their expectations. Even with all the confidence Abuti Ben had imparted to me, allowing me to aspire to be a world champion, I soon learned that it was a pipedream.

Now that I was finally here, the pain of not jumping on that flight was incomparable. The thought that I would be travelling abroad for the first time in my life was mind-blowing.

Having never before tackled an international flight, I got to the airport an hour before the flight was due to take off. None of my friends and family had ever flown anywhere, so no one would even know that you needed to be at the airport much earlier than that. Even as the car broke down on our way to the airport, I remained calm, thinking about the many times the taxis and buses had broken down during my years at Patricia's school. It was only after Manolo called that I realised just how fine we were cutting it. He didn't mince his words as he told me to get to the airport right away. I couldn't even admit to him that the car had broken down. I had already been delayed by a week, and a stand-in was holding my place for a week aboard the vessel as I recovered. My outbound ticket, and homeward flight for the stand-in, had already been bought.

Arriving at the airport, I sprinted to the check-in desk and was told that they had closed and that my flight was about to board. I pleaded with them to check me in, to which they relented, giving me a boarding pass and telling me to get through security as quickly as possible. Mercifully, security was smooth and I made it to the immigration desk just as quickly. Thinking that the worst was behind me and that I now had all the time in the world, I strolled around the airport duty-free shops in awe of the shining and fragrant displays of perfume and African curiosities. I saw a sign for the Air France lounge; it did not even occur to me that, with my economy ticket, I could not go there. I just assumed that was where all Air France passengers went. I presented my ticket to the receptionist, who took one look at it and knew I was on the cusp of missing my flight.

'Sir, your ticket is economy, and your flight is about to take off,' she said with a note of alarm. She told me to sprint to my gate right away, releasing me like a bat out of hell. Racing down the escalator, I approached the gate where the agent was waiting for me.

'Mr Radebe, unfortunately, you have been offloaded from this flight,' she said.

'No, I can't be.'

I dropped to my knees and began praying in sight of all the other passengers and staff in this busy wing of Africa's biggest airport. Someone helped to pick me up from the floor as I became hysterically frantic. The lady persisted that it was too late, there was nothing they could do once the aircraft door had been closed.

I kept screaming that my life was over. I was never going to get this opportunity again. Internally I was praying.

'God, if you are there, this is when I want to see your hand. I promise to be a good child if you do this one thing for me,' I said silently, pacing up and down.

Perhaps touched by my crying or praying in tongues, one of the ladies picked up the phone and called the captain. After a few minutes of pleading, she hung up, gave me a long stare and told me they would be opening the door for me after all. She told me that this should never ever happen again, as she could lose her job.

I restrained myself from hugging the air hostesses and hopped aboard the vast aircraft as fast as I could. I boarded clutching my bags as some passengers shot me dirty looks. I couldn't have cared less.

'I'm here,' I thought to myself.

And there I was, in my tight blue jeans and a white shirt with black dress shoes. I was in economy, yet dressed as though I was going to a nineties African charismatic church or to the plane's business class bar. I didn't even know where to stow my bag as all the other passengers were seated and the overhead bins were shut. I struggled to locate my seat. But I was there, and I was going to Italy. When I sat down, I cried for what felt like forever. The people next to me maintained a dignified silence and pretended to not notice my sobs.

I arrived the next morning, letting out a huge sigh of relief as my feet touched foreign soil. After collecting my checked bags and navigating immigration, I left the terminal where a middle-aged Italian man was waiting, holding a sign with my name on it. I cried when I realised that there was someone waiting for me. It was all real; I had not been scammed. The driver did not speak a word of English and I didn't speak Italian, but after a while, we both settled into our silence. I got to my room and switched on the television. It finally sunk in that this was my new life as the animated Italian voices reverberated around the suite.

I was booked into the hotel for one night before I was due to board the ship the following day. I didn't leave my hotel room that day. I was so nervous that I might put another foot wrong. I didn't speak the language and had no idea where I was. I had visions of announcing to everyone that I was leaving South Africa, and then returning with my tail between my legs. How embarrassing that would be. After my disastrous experience at the airport, I just thought, 'Get me on that bloody boat. Whatever it takes.'

I woke up early the next morning and was driven to the port. I will never forget the moment I saw the cruise ship for the first time. There it was. Majestic. It was gleaming white and enormous; a giant of the sea. Its sheer size was terrifying, and it sat proudly against the backdrop of the ocean. I had seen the sea many times at some of the competitions I had been to, but I had never stepped foot on a boat, even a wooden dinghy.

'Oh my God. I'm literally going to be living on the sea,' I thought to myself.

Along with other passengers and crew members, we clambered aboard. People were waving and kissing each other goodbye.

'Ciao! Ciao!' echoed around.

I stood in awe, taking in this hotel of the waves. It had the air of a theme park paired with a shopping centre – all shiny shops and manufactured fun. When I walked into the theatre, it was incredible and I still couldn't believe I was no longer on dry land. I had never been so excited. It was like the first day of school all over again, only this time, I had no fear. I knew who I was. And this time, I was not going to tone down or hide any part of myself. I had officially arrived.

Chapter Eight

'I Am Johannes Radebe'

Time goes by in the blink of an eye. I spent seven years on the ships, and days seemed to disappear at warp speed. In that time, I had gone from never having set foot outside South Africa to sailing the seven seas with a job that I loved. The financial security that came with it gave me the space to find myself for the first time. The fact that I was fed, had a bed at night and did a job I loved was an incredible privilege. As dancers, our job was not hard and we were not overworked. We would welcome guests, put on dance and theatre shows, and go into the dining room dressed up to the nines to have our pictures taken with guests. There were themed nights, and we would dress according to the night. I had my eyes opened to the world of musical theatre. I had no idea who ABBA was and, not long after, I was performing in *Mamma Mia!* and other shows like *The Lion King*, *Grease*, *Chicago* and *Hairspray*. We put on shows in extravagant and ornate costumes and lived our best lives.

Our relationships with guests were transitory, but I met some wonderfully interesting people, and I forged connections with people from all over the world. I was also lucky enough to go off the boat when it stopped for shore excursions. I could tag along at no cost to me. We travelled to every corner of the globe, and I had such an incredible education by participating in sightseeing activities and guided tours. From the perfect blue lagoons and powder-white sands of the French Polynesian islands to the vast cityscapes of Sydney, Rio de Janeiro and Singapore, it was a personal odyssey. All the money I made went back home to my mum via PayPal into her Western Union account.

Living on the ship also forced me to confront my own issues with intimacy and relationships. I was twenty-one when I first stepped aboard, a time by which many people have had their first romantic relationships and their initial sexual encounters. I had experienced neither at that point. In the first couple of years aboard, I was the same reclusive person I had always been on land. I avoided any relationships outside of platonic friendships.

When I did eventually open up to the idea of dating, I went out with one or two of the lads on the ship, mostly colleagues who worked in other departments. They all wanted to be subtle about their relationship with me and, though the secrecy didn't sit well with me, I reasoned that it was probably best to be discreet since the ship was like a small village where everyone knew everything about everybody else's business. I told myself that I didn't want to feed the gossip, but, deep down, I actually wanted to be acknowledged and to have a normal relationship that didn't need to be hidden. I didn't necessarily want to be a topic of conversation, but I still wanted at least one solid relationship that I could proudly own and be comfortable being part of. I craved the stability and security of a relationship over casual entanglements, insisting on spending quality time together. Most of the guys would play along for a month or two before it would fizzle out, either because they disembarked or they got tired of my reluctance to be intimate before we had established an emotional connection.

I was locked in a pattern of falling for the guys who had no interest in me while not giving the time of day to the caring ones. I was deeply insecure, which made it almost impossible to forge meaningful connections. I allowed myself to believe that I was too much to handle. Part of me still carried the shame of being bullied and picked on at school; I had always felt like the odd one out. My relationship with men was one that had been shaped by distrust and fear. This is why I would gravitate towards relationships that were doomed to fail – I knew no other way. Maybe I was stacking the odds against myself so that I didn't have to open myself up only to find myself rejected – my version of an emotional life raft.

The idea that I had to change myself to make others comfortable was one bad habit from high school that I jettisoned for good. That said, soon after joining the world of cruise ships, I continued to see with greater clarity that, paradoxically, the straighter 'acting' gay men found it far easier to date other men. It is a toxic phenomenon that exists in the community all over the world, and it confused me greatly, further hampering my self-confidence. Not only had I encountered homophobia from straight boys through school, now I was dealing with men who were queer but moved through the world as 'straight passing'.

Despite their outward heterosexual behaviours, they still wanted casual encounters with me without providing me with any of the emotional security I yearned for.

I am proud to say that I had transcended the internalised homophobia that haunts so many people coming to terms with their sexuality. There was nothing wrong with me; there was something wrong with a society that encourages people to suppress themselves to survive. I was comforted that, despite all my self-doubt, I had accepted myself and would never compromise that by trying to pass as straight.

Turning twenty-one is a rite of passage, the milestone at which you step into manhood. As I embraced that, I reminded myself to do it authentically and honestly. Dance – my bulwark against isolation and despair – had played a leading role in my confidence. All my dance teachers had instilled in me the conviction to own every move that I made on the dance floor. Dance requires bravado and so, as I contemplated who I wanted to be as I took my first steps into adulthood, I resolved to face the future with honesty, courage and conviction.

Every year I would go back home to Zamdela on annual leave. Being home for those breaks grounded me. It was always refreshing to reconnect with my old friends and my family, with the security of a job still waiting for me at sea.

Towards the end of my seventh year on the ship, I was promoted to production manager and dance captain, working with the company to cast and manage the ship's entire dance production. I was honoured to be entrusted with the responsibility and equally daunted. Being Black, young and queer in that setting came with its challenges. I found that, because I wasn't Italian and didn't speak much of the language, I sometimes struggled to fit in with the management. I was now exposed to hierarchies and politics from which I had been shielded when I was simply a dancer.

The dynamic of my relationships with some of the other dancers also shifted because of my new position. Before, we were all equal and leaned on each other as dancers. After my promotion, I would hear people talking or laughing behind my back. The ship was like a township on water and, while that brought with it incredible relationships, it could very quickly become bitchy or political. It was personally challenging, but I kept my head up and did my work. My real friends remained steadfast and supportive. It was my first real exposure to leader-ship – the ultimate double-edged sword.

Cruise ships are an industry to behold, and yet after years during which it had felt like a boundless world, it had become to feel like an island. There was only so much I could do before I hit a ceiling. I did not want to be the person who spent thirty years of their life on ships because it is not real life. Contracts ended, and people left. Lots of relationships were transitory. Undoubtedly, those seven years were some of the best of my life because I got to travel the world and meet so many people, but there were bastards in the mix and I had had enough of the politics. There was no escaping misogyny, sexism and racism. While there was a strict no-tolerance policy for these things by management on board, let's be honest, there are always one or two in a crowd who ruin it for everyone else. I got to a point where I had had enough. I felt that the time had come to put down roots and find a different sense of permanence. I also wanted a home and to win a South African dance title.

I left the cruise ship industry and flew back home, ready for a new challenge. I had saved up what I thought would be enough money to sustain me for a while, perhaps even enough for me to return to university and get a degree.

I arrived home to my mum's open arms. She was delighted to have me back. What I had not anticipated was that my savings would be depleted within three months. The financial situation at home was far worse than I had anticipated. I got back to South Africa and immediately invested in a car and set about getting a driving licence. I signed up for an intensive driving course and passed in no time at all. If I was going to rebuild my life back home, I would need the independence to go wherever I needed. I refused to be stranded again.

Being out of the country for almost a decade meant that I was out of touch with the local choreographers, so I spent those first couple of months driving all over, auditioning for any gig that seemed like a decent prospect.

I arrived at a number of auditions low on petrol, praying that whatever I had would be enough to get me back home to Zamdela. Fortunately, I was no longer afraid to ask for help. Life had taught me that if you don't ask, you don't get, and I believe most humans are instinctively helpful. Sometimes help would come from friends, and other times from what can only be characterised as divine intervention – like when my car was running on fumes.

After a while, I reached out to a few friends and Ausi Tebogo to tell them that I was back in the country and needed to be plugged in with work opportunities. At this point, I also made the decision to slow down and stop running myself ragged, going to every audition in town. It was the best decision I could have made, forcing me to stand still for a second while lifting my anxiety.

Not long after, word got around that I was back, and I started getting calls about gigs from industry friends, and Ausi Tebogo offered me teaching gigs. I was in the full swing of this new chapter when Ausi Tebogo informed me that *Strictly Come Dancing* South Africa – a franchise of the original UK version – was in pre-production for its seventh season and was looking for a new slate of dancers. *Strictly Come Dancing* launched in South Africa shortly after I had left for the ships. Ausi Tebogo, a prominent figure in the Latin and ballroom world, ended up on the show's judging panel. The fact that it was her who told me about the audition made me feel I had a fighting chance to be on the show.

I had encountered the show during breaks from my work on the ships when I would harshly critique the featured dancer.

'Oh my gosh, you could have pointed your toe better there. The arms are not supported. The feet are not quick enough,' I would yell at the TV.

Back home, Mum would look at me and tell me to put my money where my mouth was and join the show, not least because I was ruining the viewing experience for everyone else.

Most of the dancers on the show were my peers. Watching them, it was abundantly clear to me that my love for Latin American and ballroom had not diminished. On the ships, we performed the spectrum of dance genres, and the little Latin and ballroom we did was watered down. I couldn't believe that the stars were aligning in this way. Ausi Tebogo generously offered to coach me ahead of the audition. Sadly, I couldn't raise the funds to make it for the pre-audition sessions with her. I did, however, manage to pull together all my resources to make it to the audition itself.

Once there, I met the executive producer, Kee-Leen Irvine, and had a formal interview and dancing assessment. Kee-Leen told me that the job was mine. I immediately called Ausi Tebogo and thanked her for the opportunity of a lifetime. She chided me for not soliciting her advice ahead of the audition, but was delighted that I had secured the job regardless. I was overjoyed. It was so exhilarating to know that I would be on TV. I needed to go home and prepare.

My life had come full circle to be on the same show as Ausi Tebogo. Not only had she affirmed my passion for dancing all those years ago when she visited our studio in Ennerdale, she had gone on to offer me a teaching job in her studio and had now set me on my own *Strictly* path. I had honoured her advice to dance my heart out whenever I had the chance. She lived by her mantra. Ausi Tebogo was the first dancer I had seen amass a legion of fans that followed her around the country. When she and her partner, Kagiso Ntseane, took the floor, the tumult of the fans cheering would drown out the music.

Ausi Tebogo is part of the generation of dancers that followed the legendary Salome Sechele and Tyrone Watkins, one of the first Black couples to represent South Africa competitively abroad. Salome and those like her changed the trajectory and face of ballroom and Latin American dancing for Black people in South Africa. They showed us that it was possible to dance competitively and professionally at that level. They took dance from a weekend social and recreational pastime to a level where we could go out into the world and become champions – where others would sit up and take notice. Salome inspired an entire generation. Tebogo and Kagiso were hot on their heels, casting a spell on a new generation of fans like me who looked up to the ten-time dance champion and six-time South African Latin American Champion.

After calling Ausi Tebogo to inform her of my casting, the next person I called was my mother.

'Guess who's going to join *Strictly*?' I remember saying boastfully.

It came as such a lovely surprise to her. A show like *Strictly Come Dancing* changes not just the life of the participant but also that of their loved ones.

From my first appearance on the show, my mum walked around Zamdela, basking in the recognition it had brought.

'We saw your wonderful child,' her neighbours would tell her.

'How is your child?' people would ask her while she shopped.

My mother was not generally the kind of parent who proclaimed her pride from the rooftops, but it was in moments like those, and when she would walk around brandishing my trophies, that I knew she was delighted.

I was so excited to get my first taste of telly and meet the stars whom I had watched myself. All of a sudden, I was in their company, part of the same show as them, being beamed to millions of homes across South Africa. I had underestimated the impact television and a show like *Strictly Come Dancing* could have on society. It felt like I was part of a new wave of creative energy coursing through our nation. Interest in dance was high, with many studios reporting unprecedented student enrolments. It was magical to witness people talking about dance. For ten weeks, the country would be transfixed. I had grown up thinking of football, rugby, cricket and even tennis as the cool TV options, so being publicly acknowledged and having kids tell you that you are cool because you danced was surreal. It was magical. I would be extremely chuffed and emotional every time I met a fan, especially when they shared what joy the show brought them.

Strictly was a whole new world for me. Behind the scenes, it took me a long time to find my feet. Even though I knew that dance as a medium spanned platforms including TV and film, I had never really considered the prospect of working in television. I had always considered myself shy by nature, and the telly was for extroverts and people who could entertain and enthral audiences. As far as I was concerned, I was born for the stage, not the box. On the dance floor, I didn't have to open my mouth – my body did all the talking. *Strictly* was the first time I would be challenged to bring myself and my thoughts to the public arena. No longer was I playing a role, now I was speaking as myself to millions of viewers.

I was comforted by the fact that dancing filled up most of the transmission and I was, in essence, being paid to teach.

'I can teach anybody to dance, I've been doing it since forever,' I would reassure myself as I sought to calm my nerves.

That bit I knew was not the challenge. The problem was having to speak on camera, which for me was the single most frightening part of stepping into the *Strictly* studio. To some degree, this is still the case. The difference is that now I have the tools. I've learned over the years to keep both feet on the ground, my first step to centring myself. Then I quietly read the room, silently narrating what I see in the room.

'There's the couch. The monitor. My partner next to me,' I would think as I concentrated on my breathing and presence, finding my place of clarity and calmness. To this day, I still find this part of being on TV hard. It is a process, and it feels like a big responsibility. I knew then that I would need to use tools, like breathing, to help. I applaud the people who are very comfortable in front of the camera.

My first season of *Strictly* was one of my hardest but also one of the best for inducting me into the storied show's culture. I count myself lucky to have absorbed it as early as I did because it has made a world of difference to my time on the show as well as my relationships with my partners.

I walked into *Strictly* that first year armed with what I had learned during my many years of competitions. In my mind, the singular goal was to win – this was, after all, the world of wins and losses, judges and trophies. I soon came to realise that the show was about so much more than that. *Strictly* is about telling stories, it's about transformation, a journey from A to B; it's about bringing joy, hope and entertainment. It's an entertainment show first and foremost, with competition just the garnish. This hard lesson would take a couple of years to sink in.

My first partner on the South African show was the wonderful singer and activist LeAnne Dlamini. I was beyond thrilled to be paired with her. She was an admired singer who knew how to get down to a beat. That said, LeAnne and I didn't start our relationship on a high note.

I had gone into the rehearsal room ready to push us to the finish line. I had it all figured out in my head, complete with a plan for how it was going to go down. I was new to the show and had still not worked out the real mechanics. Instead of walking in with an open mind and heart, I walked in ready to compete. I wanted to win at all costs. Clearly, I had neglected the crux of the show: the celebrity embarking on their journey into dance. These were not championships at which we would be vying for a title. This was about bringing joy to millions of viewers, an opportunity to ignite a love of dance in my non-professional dancer partner.

I regret to say that I bled the joy out of the process in those first few weeks. We trained so hard that there was no enjoyment to be had. It began to dawn on me that LeAnne might actually be hating this experience and, while I was used to dancing for twelve hours a day, she was not necessarily going to be on board with that idea. It was then that I resolved to change my approach and began consulting with my other professional dancer friends on the show.

'What am I doing wrong? It seems like I can't get through to my partner,' I pleaded.

Mercifully, help was readily offered.

Strictly judge Harold Van Buuren came to our rehearsal room to help manage the mounting tension. LeAnne's husband, Sipho Dlamini, also came to spend time with us in the studio and, over time, I grew so fond of Sipho that I secretly wished he was the one with whom I was competing.

I admired Sipho and LeAnne's love and devotion for each other and could tell Sipho wanted his wife to do well. I was impressed that he put his life on hold to mediate. It was beautiful to see their love and how level-headed Sipho was as he brokered peace between us. I came to understand LeAnne's creative process and that she and I were in this together. It was only then that I finally understood I needed to see my partner as a human and not just a dancer. The truth is that I had pushed her to a point at which it had become an unbearable experience not only for her but for me as well. This was an enormous learning curve. I had convinced myself this was what the format demanded, but I was so very wrong. The camera would roll as we confronted difficult moments in rehearsals. Both being South African meant that LeAnne and I could be quite confrontational. South Africans, unlike the British, haven't mastered the art of sarcasm. We tend to tackle things head-on, very directly, with little in the way of cushioning or dry humour. LeAnne opened my eyes to the realities of being an artist and being in show business, and learning to be kind in the process.

I had to consider that it really wasn't about lifting the glitterball trophy or standing in front of the monitor awaiting the judges' scores; it was instead about the experience. I decided to lean into the fun side of the process and let go of the precision.

From that point, LeAnne and I not only excelled on the floor, but our relationship grew stronger right through to the season finale. Jonathan Boynton-Lee, a television presenter on one of South Africa's leading TV shows, *Top Billing*, walked away with the *Strictly* glitterball after wooing the country with steamy moves and a six-pack moment that had us screaming our lungs out both at home and in the studio. How did we ever stand a chance against Jonathan's ripped abs?

We wrapped up the seventh season of *Strictly*, my first as a participant, on a high. Alongside LeAnne, the other stars included actress and socialite Khanyi Mbau, actor and TV host Siv Ngesi and media personality Boity Thulo. After my time with them, I felt hopeful about the future. This fascinating world of glitz, glamour and A-listers was giving me confidence about my return.

After all my years of competing aggressively, the show was teaching me that it wasn't always about me and how good I was. Therein lies the genius of the format – both the celebrity and the professional dancer are judged as one, even though they are technically on different scales. Nothing is more humbling than to be asked to step outside of yourself and consider yourself as part of a team. It was a lesson not only in how to teach, but how to build empathy. Even though LeAnne and I didn't win the season, we still walked away the best of friends and hugely proud of our journey. She is still a sister, someone whom I cherish more than words can express.

In South Africa, *Strictly Come Dancing* guaranteed work for just one-quarter of the year. And so it was that, two months after the show finished, I found myself on a downward spiral. Anxiety slowly crept in as it dawned on me that I hadn't planned for what would come next. Yes, I was now on TV, but your ego can never be the prize. I don't think that works for anyone. Now I know that if you work hard and are kind, your phone will never stop ringing. I wish I had known then that I could trust the process. I was only just beginning to surround myself with people who would nurture me and help. I was starting to see that, when I called people and told them of my predicament, they would always lend a helping hand in any way that they could.

Gripped by uncertainty, my friend Jane Fry came to the rescue again and invited me to stay with her to clear my mind. At that time, I was contemplating a career change, once again considering going back to university, but my finances were still a hindrance. I was at a crossroads and thinking hard about leaving dance completely. I was still doing the odd corporate gig or wedding, but it was not enough. I split my time between Jane's house in Bryanston, north Johannesburg, and my mum's in Zamdela. On the days when I was at Jane's, she would return from work and we would talk at length about possible next steps. While there were times I found it hard, I always felt it would work out for me.

In the end, it was Jane who came up with the plan for me to join *Burn the Floor*, one of the world's leading Broadway and West End productions, and the ultimate stage production for professional Latin and ballroom dancers. *Burn the Floor* was distinguished for casting a stellar collection of dancers who were international title holders – the best of the best.

Having watched the stage production on DVD, Jane was convinced that I would be well suited for the show. Seeing how amped up Jane was, I began to research the show. I discovered that the only other South African male dancer to have joined the production was Keo Motsepe, who went on to join the American cast of *Dancing with the Stars*.

Keo was an impressive dancer who had reigned as the South African champion eleven times. To join *Burn the Floor*'s cast, hopefuls needed to be a world dance champion or have some international recognition, which came as a body blow. If I'd had access to all the resources necessary for grooming, I believe I could have won the South African professional championships and perhaps even the world championships. But the odds were always stacked against me. Now here I was once again, about to miss out on another opportunity. I was despondent, defeated.

After talking to Jane, we decided that I should reach out to the company anyway and try my luck. I spent the next couple of days asking everyone I knew for an email address for the team. I drew a blank. Then Jane had the idea to look at the back of her DVD and there, on the credits, was an email address. We decided to go online to google the names of the creative team, going as far as checking their LinkedIn profiles. We came across associate producer Peta Roby's contacts, so I sent her a one-line email at 11pm: 'I am Johannes Radebe, a dancer from South Africa. I would love to be a part of *Burn the Floor*,' I wrote.

A couple of weeks went by, and I moved on and forgot about the email. Then, one afternoon, I opened my emails and Peta had replied, requesting my showreel. I put together a couple of clips from shows I did on the ships as well as the season of *Strictly* I had just wrapped. That was the only Latin and ballroom reference I had at the time because of the seven years I had just spent on the ships doing non-Latin and ballroom styles.

Though they could tell that I could dance, *Burn the Floor* was first and foremost a Latin and ballroom outfit, and so it wasn't enough to see me doing other styles. However, my showreel did pique their interest. In their reply, they requested footage of me dancing with a professional dancer and not a just celebrity on *Strictly*. Undeterred, I thought 'fair enough, back to the dance floor'. It had been more than eight years since I last competed, and I did not have any old footage. I called Ausi Tebogo and she agreed to coach me for my return to the South African national championships.

We had a month before the two federation competitions. For upwards of fourteen hours a day, I rehearsed under Ausi Tebogo's eagle eye. She gave up her time because she understood what I needed to achieve. I would be competing for not only the title but also as an audition for *Burn the Floor*. My partner, Jeanne Swart, wanted a solid dance career, so she invested everything into the process. Our hard work paid off when we won both national championship titles under the professional section that year.

By June 2014, I was a two-time national champion in South Africa. That was my pitch to *Burn the Floor* when I emailed them back: 'I would like to inform you that I'm now the reigning South African champion,' I wrote, attaching clips from the competitions, waiting with bated breath for their response.

Peta congratulated me and said they had a job for me. As my disbelief turned to euphoria, I got another call from Kee-Leen, my boss from *Strictly*, inviting me for another season. I inhaled before calmly thanking Kee-Leen, but telling her that I had just been offered a great opportunity to join the international cast of *Burn the Floor*. She wished me well and said she was sad to see me go, particularly after the success of my last season with LeAnne, making it to the finals.

Burn the Floor offered me a contract to join them on one of their three cruise lines as none of their shows was touring on land at that time, to which my heart sank. This was a Latin and ballroom dancer's dream – to get a foot in the door at a company like that – but I had just got away from the ships, only to be told I would be going right back there. In the end, we decided I would return to *Strictly* for another season and then join *Burn the Floor* when they came to South Africa later as part of their world tour. I still had a shot at the opportunity of a lifetime.

Chapter Nine

It Takes a Village

I was thrilled to be back on *Strictly* South Africa, now knowing what awaited me when we wrapped. *Burn the Floor* would be the happiest of landings. I was paired with the delightful Capetonian television and radio host, Leigh-Anne Williams.

Having learned the secrets of a successful journey on the show, I approached my second run with deliberate calm and an open heart. We hit it off immediately. The show continued to woo audiences across the country, with incredible ratings every week. Leigh-Anne and I remained firmly atop the leader board until the finals. As well as helping me settle into the rhythm and workings of the show, Leigh-Anne opened me to learning and exchanging energy and ideas. I no longer sought to be the unquestioned leader-teacher. I was just as open to learning something new. Leigh-Anne would go on to offer me much-needed media training. Working in the industry, she was a natural when it came to handling herself in front of cameras and audiences. She drilled me on how to keep things classy and poised. No longer was I the impulsive and unrefined Johannes from the previous season. Where I come from, people say what they think. I had learned to take my time and think before I opened my mouth. She exuded such tranquillity that she made me feel comfortable enough to make mistakes without fearing judgement. That was one of her strongest traits, along with how she lit up the room with her effervescence. I learned so much from her over those ten weeks. Leigh-Anne and I made it to the final rounds and went head-to-head with the season winner, Afrikaans pop sensation, Karlien van Jaarsveld and partner Devon Snell. It was a tough route to the finish line. We were the runners-up for the glitterball, and I couldn't have been prouder of our journey. Receiving that much support from the entire country was truly reaffirming.

A couple of weeks later, *Burn the Floor* arrived in South Africa for their tour. They announced my casting in the show, releasing my name and pictures to the media nationwide. It was by far my biggest career moment at that point. It felt even more special because it confirmed South Africa as the home of world-class talent, with me as the third South African to join the cast and only the second Black, male dancer.

I will never forget the pride on my mother's face when she saw my feature on *Top Billing*, a hugely popular Saturday evening magazine show. It was must-watch TV. The group that had nurtured my talent and groomed me all those years ago also took great pride in the moment. It was something for all of us to celebrate and cherish. I got on the phone with Uncle Elvis, Aunt Patricia and Ausi Mpho, and said a little prayer for Abuti Ben, who had passed on a few years earlier. I also thanked Ausi Tebogo for her contribution to my journey. All those years of hard graft were finally paying off. Jane and I jumped for joy.

Booking *Burn the Floor* was just the tonic I needed after two years of fretting about my future. In between the seasons of *Strictly*, I had experienced bouts of depression, beating myself up for dropping out of college and worrying that my career back in South Africa was unsustainable. This negative internal monologue really harmed my mental health. Looking at my home situation and my responsibility to look after the family piled on pressure to attain financial freedom. I was the breadwinner at home and the 'Black tax' – the pressure on those from disadvantaged communities to take care of others – was real; as many South Africans from homes like mine will tell you, it is a reality you do not choose and cannot escape.

In those days when I felt the walls closing in on me, there was never a doubt in my mind that providing for my family was my responsibility. When it would get too much, I would lock myself away, feeling despondent and as though I had nothing valuable to offer the world. There is nothing worse than living with that kind of pressure on your shoulders. People don't talk enough about this weight, which can be all-consuming, draining your life force – particularly when you don't have the reassurance that everything will work out for the best. Studying is not an option for you. Starting a business requires capital that you don't have. The only way out might be an entry-level job, that may or may not have anything to do with your passions and talents, taking you away from the same family you are working so hard to provide for.

From the day my dad died, I understood that it was no longer about me, it was about family. You block out a lot of trauma in

order to move through life and cope. As a child, I couldn't articulate the love–hate relationship that I had with my father. On
the one hand, I knew that I was besotted with him, he was my
everything. On the other hand, I hated what he did to my
mother. To us. And it was only as an adult that I could admit
how much his death had upset me. I was angry at him. I blamed
him for putting us in the situation that we were left in. I couldn't
understand how he could suddenly decide to die.

I never spoke to anyone about my feelings, believing there
was nobody to whom I could speak candidly. He had caused so
much pain and disappointment to so many people. Even when
I wanted to celebrate our beautiful memories, I felt like I had no
one to talk to because he had messed things up with everyone
else so monumentally. I didn't think Mum would delight in
reminiscing fondly about him after the pain she had endured. I
buried my emotions about my father with him, keeping most of
it covered up deep within me.

When I finally realised that my dream of joining *Burn the Floor*
was about to come true I wept, releasing the anxiety I had been
carrying in the years since I came back from sea. I cried for the
loss of my father. I cried for having to admit that his loss had hit
me so hard. I cried for everything. I discharged all the bad and all
the losses. I wept for the little boy who had to be a man before he
was ready; the university student who had to drop out of school
when all he wanted was a degree like Aunt Martha; the young
man who had struggled to make ends meet. I made peace with
the younger me who had put everything aside, including his
emotions, and gone into the world to make something of himself.

Joining the cast of *Burn the Floor* was another chance to finally get back to a solid income to support my family. The world tour would take me as far afield as Japan, Australia and India. I was partnered with an Australian dancer named Megan, a classy angel in human form. I felt like God was looking down on me and knew just how much I needed someone with a good heart and a healthy outlook at that point in my journey. We hit it off and remained partners for the entire season.

My first show with the cast was at the Joburg Theatre in South Africa, and was unlike anything in my career to that point. My people turned up in buses, taxis and convoys to see me unveiled as the newest member of the cast. Mum and Aunt Martha were part of the bus that came from Sasolburg to support me that night.

My moment arrived three minutes into the show. The choreographers were so clever in making small alterations to the show for every city we toured. Because of my following and all the media attention my casting had received in South Africa, they choreographed an entire entrance for my first step on stage. To the beat of Rihanna's 'Don't Stop the Music', the lights went off and, when they came back on, I samba-ed on stage from the wings to an instrumental dance break in the song arrangement. The Joburg Theatre erupted with cheers and screams. My childhood friends, industry backers, legends I admired, *Strictly* castmates and family were packed into the theatre. It was a moment of sheer pride and joy. That moment that night was not about 'Johannes Radebe', it was about the entire force behind those cheers which said, 'One of us is on the international stage.' I was now on a par with the best in the world. I was proud to be a part of that moment.

I knew that no matter what happened moving forward, I could find peace knowing that I had fulfilled my dreams. I had gone to the heights Abuti Ben had mythologised when I was a little boy. This was the first time in my life when I said a heartfelt 'well done' to myself. I had a moment of self-introspection about my dancing career in which I affirmed myself for the first time. I had stuck it out, and it was at that moment that I knew I had been right all along – dance was my calling.

After our Johannesburg run, we toured Australia, Japan and the UK. Unlike *Strictly*, *Burn the Floor* was a fiercely competitive world, something which I initially found a challenge to readjust to. Everyone on the show was a world dance champion title holder. I was working with the finest dancers in Latin and ballroom dancing. There were times when I felt pangs of insecurity because I only came with my South African titles. Yet most dancers on the show were also on edge, ready to defend their titles with every move and every show.

After a spell of feeling thrown off balance by the show's heavily competitive nature, I made my peace and responded by dancing with my heart again and getting out of my mind.

Living out of suitcases in foreign cities for nearly three years was an interesting experience. I was thrilled to learn that we would be going to the West End with the production. It was this dancer's dream to step onto the vaunted stages of Broadway in

New York City and London's West End. For our run in the UK, we rehearsed at the Dominion Theatre, where *The Bodyguard* was showing. It was incredible to see Alexandra Burke glide through the theatre and to catch glimpses of her in rehearsals. At that time, I also bumped into Beverley Knight, whose single 'Gold' was a staple of South African radio. If bumping into the Beverley Knights and Alexandra Burkes of this world was to be a regular occurrence in this town, then London was where I wanted to be.

This was only my second time in London and my first actually visiting for more than a day. When I worked for the cruise line we would sometimes dock in Southampton and be taken by bus to visit Covent Garden and Buckingham Palace as a quick excursion before returning to the ship. Now back in London with *Burn the Floor*, I found myself booked in a hotel room off Kingsway and walking to the Peacock Theatre where the show was running. I couldn't believe we were having a run in the West End. This was a big deal.

Our London show had upped the ante within the already competitive cast. Rumours swirled that top BBC bosses were coming to watch. After the South African show, I had been rechoreographed back into the ensemble, with my one key solo in the middle of the show. My partner Megan and I spoke briefly about the situation, having felt the energy shift backstage. People were looking to be scouted for other opportunities. Megan and I continued with the same level of energy, focus and commitment as we'd brought to the rest of the tour. We were neither going to risk underperforming nor overdoing it, which might end up with us being out of sync. We had some of our best shows in London.

One night, after a particularly sparkling show, the cast was invited for drinks with the line-up of that year's *Strictly Come Dancing* who had been in the audience. I reconnected with Oti Mabuse, who had become a household name in Britain and a *Strictly* audience favourite. Not many people know that Oti and I came up together on the South African competitive circuit. During my time at Ausi Tebogo's studio, Oti and I even tried out to see if we could partner each other. She went on to get her break in Germany, following her big sister, Motsi. Back in London, we had a lovely evening with the *Strictly* dancers.

In the next day's papers, the reviews were out and one shrewdly pointed out that a girl with pink hair and a tall Black man had set the stage alight. I couldn't believe my eyes. We had received our first West End thumbs up! I have held on to that newspaper clipping to this day and thanked my angels for my continued good fortune.

After London, we toured the entire country, taking in Manchester, Liverpool, Brighton and more. As that tour ended, I got a contract to join *Burn the Floor*'s seagoing cast again. They sent me a heart-warming email in which they said they wanted my expertise on their team. The contract even included 'passenger access' – meaning I could eat at all the fine dining restaurants on board; a definite step up from what I was used to. As a sought-after West End production, we had a lot of perks on the ship.

It was mid-contract when I received a call from Kee-Leen from South Africa, offering me a spot on the first season of *Dancing with the Stars South Africa*. The show was moving to another channel, under a new brand, and Kee-Leen said she would love to have me back. She made me an offer I couldn't refuse and I returned home, much to *Burn the Floor*'s disappointment.

I was paired with Vanes-Mari du Toit, a woman with a big heart and, for the first time, a partner who was even taller than me. Vanes is a netball star on the South African national team and was at the peak of fitness. Together we danced our hearts to the semi-finals and even wider acclaim and recognition. After about three years away, I realised how much I had missed home. I have always loved being home, but have had to look further afield to earn a crust as a dancer. I had always dreamed of being home and closer to Mum, my family and friends.

It was while I was back home filming *Dancing with the Stars* that Kee-Leen and her co-producer husband Duncan informed me that BBC executives were coming all the way from London to see the show, telling me privately that they had expressed interest in meeting with me. I met executive producer Louise Rainbow and senior commissioning editor Jo Wallace, nervous but thrilled to be at the same table as them. How many people get an opportunity to sit down with the driving forces behind the mothership, *Strictly Come Dancing* UK?

They asked if I was familiar with the UK version of the show.

'Are you kidding me? Is that even a question?' I said without thinking.

Louise peered at me quizzically, and I realised that my feeble attempt at humour had not landed. I took a breath as I studied her face and realised that she was serious.

'Yes, of course. I'm familiar with the show. It is the show we all reference not only because it's the original format, but the production is so much bigger in the UK,' I blabbered.

Our conversation did not last long, and I left the table without any promises from them. I returned home and waited. The season I was working on in South Africa wrapped on 23 March 2018.

My phone finally rang over a month later on my birthday and they told me that I was being invited on to *Strictly* UK. It was the best birthday gift anyone could have ever given me, but, to my disappointment, I was sworn to secrecy until the broadcaster made the official announcement on 31 May 2018, a full month later. I, of course, told my mum, the only other soul I let in on my secret. As we enjoyed my cake that day, we winked mischievously at each other, knowing full well that we were celebrating more than just my birthday.

The day *Strictly Come Dancing* finally announced the news, I was sitting alone in a branch of a restaurant chain called Doppio Zero in Rosebank. I had an inkling that my life was about to change beyond recognition – a feeling I cannot put into words, but one I will never forget. When I got my spot in *Burn the Floor*, I thought that would be the high-water mark of my career. Now *Strictly Come Dancing* UK had taught me a valuable lesson – never curtail your dreams.

I spent the day answering calls from what felt like everyone I had ever met. Abuti Ben's family, neighbours in Sasolburg, dancers I grew up competing with, my colleagues on the ship and my entire family all wanted to speak to me. *Strictly* had organised a press tour in Johannesburg and Cape Town, and Oti was flown down to shoot a local commercial alongside me to promote the show to South African audiences.

Both Oti and I sat down with local journalists for a raft of interviews, and then I got on with the task of securing a visa and looking for somewhere to live in the UK. My professional dance partner Jeanne organised my first PR photoshoot. Since we won our titles, Jeanne had become like a sister to me. It was a wonderful congratulatory gift and equipped me with the headshots I would need for all the media requests I was fielding. Before I left, I decided to take a drive and visit all the people who had played an indelible part in my journey to thank them with all my heart. It had taken a village.

Chapter Ten

Fab-u-lous

I arrived in London in July 2018 on a hot summer's day, having left South Africa in the middle of our winter. I was surprised by how stifling London could get, considering England's reputation for bad weather. The BBC had arranged a driver to meet me at the airport and a kind gentleman with a ready smile and a firm handshake greeted me as I came through Arrivals. He offered to help with my bags, which I declined, knowing how heavy they were. He insisted, saying it was his job and that it was his pleasure after I had had a long journey. He had an easy way about him and delighted in telling me how much he loved driving the *Strictly* lot and their BBC crew, gushing about what a lovely bunch they were. I was surprised by how much he seemed to know about me and South Africa. It was hugely reassuring to meet someone so lovely from the outset of my time in London. This man's warm welcome made me feel so important, and his open face is still etched in my memory to this day.

We drove to Kensal Green, where I had signed a six-month lease on a flatshare, and my two housemates, two beautiful girls, had hidden a key for me. Sweet things that they were, they had also left a note with instructions and tips for the local area and said that they were looking forward to seeing me after work.

I walked into the cosy three-bedroom ground-floor flat, and I was immediately struck by the tiny kitchen. I had never thought it possible that there could be a kitchen smaller than Mum's, let alone in a wealthy country like Britain. My room was at the end of the hallway, with a broken door that opened to the small, charming front garden that stretched around the property.

Needing to feel immediately at home and begin adjusting to my new surroundings, I unpacked my bags. I always carry around pictures of my family: a photo of me, my mum, dad and sister together and pictures of me and Aunt Martha together. I take those pictures everywhere. I also always have a comb with me so I can brush out my hair. As a child, my mum would say to me, 'Whenever you are feeling low, take a shower and comb out your hair and it will set you up for the day.' She is always right.

After a quick shower, I ventured out in search of something to eat. The sight of the red London buses gave me a shiver of excitement.

'I am in London!' I whispered to myself.

I wanted to touch a red bus, but quickly realised how odd that would look to onlookers, so I pinched myself to check that it wasn't all a dream.

It was a couple of weeks until *Strictly* rehearsals were due to start, and I had nothing fixed to do until then. I was tempted to go galivanting in my new hometown, but felt apprehensive as I didn't know the city, so I erred on the side of caution.

Cha-cha-cha! Week 2 of Strictly (Season 19) with John Whaite

Semi-finals: our Couple's Choice performance

Winning the Media Moment of the Year award with John at the 2022 British LGBT Awards

Giving the keynote speech at Buckingham Palace to celebrate the Duke of Edinburgh's Award (2022)

Mum and me at the Palace for the Duke of Edinburgh's Award

Blackpool – dancing to Cilla Black with my Ellie in Season 20 of Strictly

Wearing two hats for my first appearance on Graham Norton (2022)

Launching House of Jojo at the London Palladium!

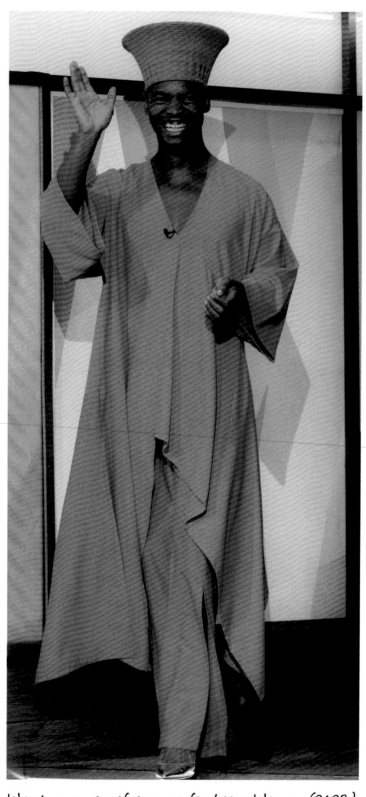

Wearing a pop of orange for Loose Women (2023)

Cover shoot for
HELLO!
(2022)

Me, mum and my
sister in Trafalgar
Square, shooting
for HELLO!

Me today – thriving!

For about a week before rehearsals, I found myself mostly alone in the flat. During the day, everyone would go to work and, in the evenings, they would be out socialising, typical for London in summer when the sun can be out late into the evening. To pass the time I would work out to physically prepare for the season ahead and watch some telly to catch up with current affairs in England.

It wasn't long before I started hearing eerie sounds in the house, and for longer than I'm prepared to admit I couldn't figure out the source of what sounded like paranormal noises. Then, one morning, I waltzed into the bathroom to brush my teeth, happily humming my favourite Tina Turner song 'Red Doll', and opened the bathroom cabinet to get my toothpaste. A massive rat jumped out and landed on my face. I screamed a blood-curdling scream and flicked the fat rat off my face as I leapt towards the main door. When I had calmed down, I snuck back inside the house and grabbed my phone to call the girls. For whatever reason, neither answered all morning. I spent half the day trapped outside, afraid to go back inside. The next person I called was my mum.

'Mum, the funny sounds are not spirits. The house is rat-infested!' I announced, half laughing, half still gasping for air.

Mum was well aware of my rat phobia. I wouldn't have minded an encounter with a lion, all sorts of reptiles or grizzly bears. Just don't give me a rat or a mouse.

'What are you going to do? You are going to come home, right?' she said innocently, with love.

Even as my life underwent the seismic changes heralded by my *Strictly* contract, Mum still made it clear that home was somewhere I could always return if needed – even if the biggest challenge facing me at that point was a rat. I reassured her that I was fine and would not be coming home just yet – it was just one of those situations that I would have to figure out. I didn't have a budget that would allow me to move out and, anyway, I was new to London. Where could I go? I hadn't yet built solid relationships with anyone.

After hours of involuntary sunbathing, afraid to be in the company of my furry friends, I went to the next-door neighbour and knocked on their door. When the door swung open, a man stared at me with a puzzled look, clearly wondering who this tall Black man was standing in his doorway. I introduced myself as his new downstairs neighbour and told him that I had a bit of an issue. Realising he hadn't yet shut the door in my face, I wasted no time and proceeded to tell him that I was petrified of rats and had just discovered a huge one downstairs.

After my panicked monologue, he smiled, and I could see he was obviously stifling a laugh.

'Are you having a laugh, mate?' he said.

Still getting acquainted with the London accent, I asked him to repeat himself.

'Are you having a laugh, mate?' he probed again.

'No, I'm not. I'm sorry to disturb you, but I would be most appreciative if you could please help me get rid of it,' I pleaded, increasingly desperate.

Perhaps it was how visibly shaken I was or he realised this would be the only way to get rid of me, but my baffled neighbour offered to come downstairs with me to assess the situation.

After a walkabout during which he peeped under my bed, moved tables and climbed on chairs, he told me the rats had probably escaped to their hideout. He explained how to report a rat infestation in a house in England, suggesting the council needed to be called and they would come to sort it out. After speaking to the girls, the council was eventually called, and their officers came to the house later that day.

As I had suspected, they confirmed that there were not one or two rats, but many. They offered us a quotation for decontamination and went away.

It was a bumpy ride from there onwards. My housemates were hardly ever home. As well as work, they also had social lives. I felt like I lived alone, and this was a stark difference to the bustling, busy households I had been used to in the past. Except for my vermin company, it was frequently just me. There were times I thought it would not work, but I always reminded myself that I had to make do. I had managed to do this my entire life in different ways. If I could get used to always being on top of other people, I should try to enjoy a bit of solitude, however unfamiliar it felt.

The first day of rehearsals with *Strictly Come Dancing* UK finally arrived. Our rehearsals that first year kicked off in central London when, from July to August, we would be rehearsing and workshopping the entire season's big numbers and show offerings. The live show went out from September to mid-December. In January, we rehearsed for the tour and kicked off the six-week *Strictly* roadshow from January to February, followed by the Pro Tour that ended around May. This meant that *Strictly* offered nine months of work a year – a thrilling prospect for any working dancer.

On my first day of rehearsals, I arrived feeling enormously grateful. Over and above the thrill of being part of the magical *Strictly* team for the foreseeable future, I was floored by rubbing shoulders with the very characters I used to study when I worked on the South African version of the show.

I lost my mind when I saw Anton. The man is a legend. There was Aljaž, looking cute as always. Janette who is super talented. Karen, who I wouldn't want to cross. Gorka is one of the most honest and genuine people you will ever meet. Neil, the prankster. Dianne, the happy chick you need in your corner to brighten your day. There was kind Amy and then, of course, lovely Luba – but don't mess with her. I felt like I knew these people long before I joined the show. The Latin and ballroom professional world is very insular. Amy and Neil were world champions and I knew of them even before *Strictly*. The biggest thing for me was also being in the same room as Oti Mabuse. Coming from South Africa, I had admired her journey and what she had achieved on the global stage. It was also comforting to have someone to speak my native South African Sesotho with. She was the closest thing I had to home, and she immediately looked out for me and was a great friend as I acclimatised. If ever there was a moment when I felt like I had arrived, it was being in the room with these and many other incredible dancers. No award or amount of money could ever compare to the feeling of seeing them practise their craft in person.

They had not secured a partner for me before I set off for London, having made it clear there was no guarantee I would get one during my first season. Although I had done the format before in my home country and I had twice made it to the finals, I did not feel it was a demotion. I was happy to have the opportunity to learn from the sidelines and to see how different the mechanics of the show were in the UK. It didn't matter that I was standing at the back for group numbers.

'Jesus, we are breathing the same air. I am fully here for it,' I thought to myself on more than one occasion.

I was far more worried about commuting to and from work and the nocturnal activities in my house than I was about anything connected to *Strictly* in those first six months. We worked hard, learning new choreography every day, but it is such a well-oiled machine that I felt so well cared for from the start.

When *Strictly* rehearsals kicked off, I hatched a plan to travel home with a speaker from which I would blast out a strong Spanish Flamenco dance as I approached the house to let my four-legged furry friends know I was home and that it was now my turn to own enjoy the communal space. I never again used the kitchen after my discovery. There was no way of knowing if our food was being scavenged when we were at work or, God forbid, something would again pounce on me. Instead, I lived on Chinese takeaways because they were tasty and cheap. I would budget £15 every day for chicken and rice or noodles. On weekends I spoilt myself and set aside an additional £5 to get a bottle of wine from the convenience store so that I could drift off and forget about the noises. Over time, I also made a draught excluder to stop them from getting under the door. I looked for a sponge and some material and stuffed it all inside a pair of long tights. When I left in the mornings, I would put it against the gap at the bottom of the door outside and, when I returned, I would move it inside, giving myself some peace of mind that they wouldn't crawl under the door.

Outside of the show, I also had to adapt to public transport in London – particularly during rush hour – as well as navigating the British tabloid media. I discovered that I am very claustrophobic and, as well as dealing with that, I worried about germs when I was travelling. You can now imagine the challenge of having to deal with commuting to work in the mornings in that first year. *Strictly* operates on a week-long schedule, mostly with days that begin at 9am and finish around 5pm – putting me slap bang in the middle of both rush hours. There were times when I had to jump off at the next stop and wait for the next Tube train, praying that it would not be as packed as the previous one and that I would not have my face in a stranger's scalp. I remember once I got stuck underground and it felt like an eternity until we got going again and arrived at the next station.

'Oh God, it's 5 o'clock. It's the evening peak and we are going to be squashed like sardines on the Bakerloo line,' would be my daily internal dialogue when my commuting anxiety attack would hit.

As summer gave way to autumn, our launch episode was finally ready to air on 8 September 2018. In true *Strictly* style, the opening and group numbers were getting bigger and more extravagant with each season.

For that year, the opening number was filmed in central London, outside the BBC's New Broadcasting House, bringing the area to a standstill as fans packed in to watch us film. I was stunned by how big the production was. There were hundreds of crew members and creatives running the show. It was a production on a scale I had never witnessed before. Adorned in black and shimmering gold costumes, the full cast, including the professional dancers, the *Strictly* band, hosts and judges, danced to a medley of hit songs, including hits like CHIC and Nile Rodgers' 'Everybody Dance' and 'Let's Dance', Diana Ross' 'I'm Coming Out' and 'We Are Family' by Sister Sledge. The opening was electrifying – we had Nile Rodgers as a surprise guest performing alongside us, and judge Anton Du Beke suspended in the air on top of a glitter ball. Little Jojo from Zamdela quietly laughed at the magic of having gay anthems like 'I'm Coming Out' and 'We Are Family' for my debut. This was the first time I would step on to the *Strictly* stage; talk about a fitting soundtrack.

In the next episode, Graziano Di Prima, Luba Mushtuk and I were officially introduced and welcomed to the show. To the sexy sounds of the *Strictly* band belting out Camila Cabello's 'Havana', the three of us took to the stage alongside the *Strictly* professionals on a Cuban-style set complete with a vintage red Plymouth Fury and palm trees. It was a steamy night at a packed, low-lit Havana bar as we set the dance floor alight, swinging our hips and shaking our bodies atop chairs, tables and whatever surface our feet landed on. The scene started with Luba in a lacy crop top and a short white tussle skirt pulling the camera inside the mysterious bar with sexy drinkers going about their business. She salsa-ed and glided across the bar, luring everyone to dance with her – but not committing to any one suitor. After casting a spell on the crowd with her captivating solo, she pulled the camera to me. I wore a white linen outfit while standing astride a table. I was the baddie who got the party started.

I had a solo that led to a couple's section with professional dancer Nadiya Bychkova. Midway through the song, the music stopped to reveal Graziano's moment. Startled by the new stranger and the music cutting out, the smoky bar came to a standstill as Graziano took a couple of paso doble steps forward, commanding our attention with an unbuttoned shirt and an air of mysterious Latin bravado. After a few seconds, the music resumed, and it was back to 'Murder on the Dance Floor'. The routine stayed centred on me, Graziano and Luba. We broke into a group dance-off between the male cast and the women. Then the music hit a crescendo to lead us to a dance break that saw us coupled again as we salsa-ed, bent our backs, turned and made room for a final dance break. This time around, it was instrumentals only, as the *Strictly* professionals broke into a final dance section, leading to the three of us stepping back to the centre and hitting our final mark for the final note. It was everything I dreamed it would be and more.

Shortly after that life-changing moment, I learned that our first musical act for that season was Gladys Knight. I thought they meant the *Strictly* live band would back us up. But midway through a rehearsal, someone mentioned a session on Friday *with* Gladys and it dawned on me what was happening. I only believed it when Gladys Knight walked in.

She was in high spirits and so humble that I plucked up the courage to come out of my shell to speak to her. I couldn't believe it when she thanked the team for our hard work at the end of our day of filming – I was already singing her lines to 'End of the Road' back to her, much to her amusement. This woman, whose music had been a soundtrack to my life from as early as I can remember, was thanking *us*. It should have been us thanking her. From my childhood going to church with my grandmother Mme and my neighbours playing her music on full blast on their verandas on Sunday mornings, Gladys Knight's music had been there. Her music was as relevant then as it is today in South Africa. Gladys is the kind of legend whose hits have transcended generations to still retain a regular mainstay on major radio stations, maintaining her standing alongside the likes of Beverley Knight and the R&B and soul stars of today. To work alongside her was a big moment for me. The picture of me and her standing behind the set at *Strictly* doesn't lie. In it, you can see my adoring reaction.

Strictly Come Dancing UK had brought so many firsts. I had my first exclusive profile with *Hello!* magazine, a publication that is widely distributed around the world and was seen by friends in all corners of the globe. I was invited to my first London Fashion Week and attended many A-list occasions, including the BAFTAs.

It was also during that first year that I received my first real media training. While Leigh-Anne Williams had taught me a thing or two about how to express myself when communicating with the media, the new spotlight that came with *Strictly* UK was about to school me into navigating the British tabloids.

In one case, my fingers were so badly burned that I was convinced I would be sent back to South Africa faster than I could say 'glitter ball'. A journalist had randomly asked me what I thought about Graziano and his celebrity partner in the show and if I thought there was chemistry between them. Taking the question at face value, I said I thought there was great chemistry between them. They were both beautiful individuals and worked hard week after week.

I got back to work the next day and my boss, the executive producer at the time, Louise, came to me and asked if I had said anything to the press about Graziano and his partner and their chemistry and – the kicker – whether I'd said they were going to fall in love. I had apparently fallen straight into a trap: talking about the so-called '*Strictly* curse'. I quickly said no, and that all I'd said was that, as a dance couple, they have amazing chemistry on the floor. To be honest, I did not know then that this was a 'thing'. I knew *Strictly* was huge over here, but I hadn't done my homework. She gave me the best advice I could have asked for on how to handle the media: never speak on behalf of other people on the show as my words, even when well-intended, could be misinterpreted.

I have remained deliberately cautious about whom I speak to in the media. It's practically impossible to fix stories that have already been published and that are out of context. All you can do most times is pray that the story dies down quickly and hope that people can identify the exaggerated bits and not draw conclusions based on tabloid angles.

As far as the *Strictly* 'curse' goes, I do not think that this phrase does the emotional side of the show justice. The beauty of my art form is that it is about more than just the dancing. It is about two souls connecting. Dancing is also about sharing, loving and taking care of one another. It is not about sex; so many relationships have been built on the show and called the *Strictly* curse, but it does create deep friendships and connections. That's the truth of it.

In December of that year, as we were preparing to wrap that year's season of *Strictly*, I received a call from *Burn the Floor* asking me to headline their UK tour alongside Graziano and Kevin Clifton. It was a no-brainer for me. *Burn the Floor* was the company that had put me on the West End stage. To have the opportunity to return to lead the production was a full-circle moment for me.

Before I could jump into that production, I returned home for Christmas at my aunt's behest, as the production took a festive break ahead of the *Strictly* tour. We filmed the last episode of *Strictly Come Dancing* in mid-December of that year and, two days after that, I jumped on a plane and flew home for two weeks. My Aunt Martha would summon the family to come home for Christmas. No one would be working, she said, so there was no reason why we shouldn't be together. We colour-coordinate our outfits and everyone brings a bowl of something, according to what they can afford. We cook braai meat and, because there were no gifts involved, all the money is put towards eating and drinking. It is always a big party. I delighted in sharing in my aunt's Christmas tradition of gathering the family for Christmas lunch and spent the New Year with my mum, my sister, nephew and niece.

On 4 January 2019, I was back in the UK for the *Strictly* tour rehearsals. Though I had danced in theatres around the world, I had never danced for a live audience of tens of thousands of people. It was intoxicating and the closest thing I will know to a being a rock star – right down to the branded tour bus and throngs of fans lining up to catch a glimpse of their favourite celebrities and dancers outside hotels and arenas. I shivered with excitement.

I come from a country where dancers are not celebrated and recognised like musicians and actors. Britain was the first place where I had seen dancers receiving the same star treatment as footballers. It was beyond heart-warming. I was overawed. I knew that I was part of a star-studded, award-winning production. I had just not clocked the size of the show's fan base, until that tour.

It was like my first time in a gay club, seeing a sea of folks who were just like me. At first, my mind couldn't process my new reality. I didn't know how to handle a world in which I was validated and seen – worthy of being celebrated and not shamed.

As I grew up, I was acutely aware of the societal stigma attached to my sexuality. But I was also exposed to just how little respect and attention was afforded to dancers and dance, often written off as merely a recreational activity. A lot of dancers, certainly of my generation, harboured a sense of shame about dance as a profession, and were never taken seriously. This motivated my obsession to get a non-dance degree all those years ago. It was both tacitly and sometimes openly encouraged to have a fall-back option.

Being on that tour challenged that. Even though I had a minor role that first year, as I had not yet been paired up, I was transformed by meeting the fans and seeing their love for dance as an art form, and dancers as athletes and artists. The best thing about touring in the UK is meeting the supporters. I always want to stop and not only extend my gratitude to the fans who are often eager to thank us, but I want to talk to them too. They are the ones who give us the courage and affirmation to do this thing that we love. They make it respectable and noble. Without them, there is no *Strictly*. I shudder to think where little Johannes would be if it was not for dancing.

During the tour, I got to see all corners of the UK. I was pleasantly surprised to discover that northerners are very much like South Africans in their sensibilities. People in the north greet each other in the streets without knowing each other, much like at home. I learned how beautiful the United Kingdom is, seeing how places like Torquay resemble Spanish coastal towns – when the sun shines. I saw coastal communities, the post-industrial heartland, mountains, hills, lakes and rivers. More than the exquisite landscapes I saw, it is the people whom I remember. There were hundreds and thousands of happy faces.

There was one occasion that blighted the positivity for a few hours. I was in Aberdeen and I was outside the venue sitting on some stairs on the phone with my mum, sipping a coffee. Thankfully, I had my belongings, including my passport, with me. As I was chatting away, a police van pulled into the parking lot where I was sitting. It slowed to a stop.

'Oh, some police are here,' I told Mum. Two officers got out of the car and started walking over.

'Mummy, they are walking over to me.'

'What did you do wrong?' she asked. I felt stung.

'Nothing.'

When they came over, I showed them my ID.

'Is there something wrong?' I asked one of them.

'No, you look suspicious and like someone we are looking out for.'

They didn't say another word and walked away.

Maybe they were doing their job, but the fact that I'd just been on stage finishing the show by myself with thousands of people shouting my name, and now I was being approached by police who thought I could be a criminal, felt like a slap in the face.

Regardless, I wrapped up the *Strictly* tour oozing positive energy and jumped straight into the *Burn the Floor* rehearsals. While taking a cast warm-up session in the first week, I accidentally kicked a table so hard that the ball of my foot could not take any pressure for days. This was a week before the opening, so I was told to observe the rehearsals and note the choreography by watching to allow my foot time to heal. The advertising for my performance in the show had already begun – it was too late to recast. I sat through so many rehearsals and my mind would race, reflecting on how quickly it could all be taken away. Before then, I never allowed an injury to stop me from doing anything. Otherwise, I would go hungry, and other people would go hungry on my watch. That was my reality.

Now I understand that these things do catch up with you. My foot was in agony, but I couldn't show it or admit it to anyone. I had worked so hard to get to a point where I was doing the kind of work I had never imagined possible. I couldn't let it slip out of my hands just as I was getting started – a fate that befalls many dancers. We are in a profession where we cannot afford injury and are repeatedly told that we have a sell-by date. After rehearsals, I would get back to the hotel and immediately plunge my foot into ice water. There were times I passed out with my foot submerged in the frozen slush. Peter, the choreographer for the show, was generous enough to adjust the choreography to ease my burden.

On opening night, I stepped onto that stage and filed away the pain, summoning the gods of dance to watch over me as I danced through the show and eventually the rest of the tour. My damaged foot carried me through until the end of the tour.

The second the tour wrapped, I flew back to Johannesburg and headed straight to the Injury Centre in Rosebank, crying all the way to the clinic. The physiotherapist told me that I would have to immediately take time off and take the weight off the foot for no less than two months. I was fortunate that nothing had broken.

The Rosebank sports rehab centre was responsible for the care and healing of professional rugby players and other top sportspeople. I underwent an intensive rehab programme to fix my foot. Thankfully, for the first time in my life, I had health insurance. Because of *Strictly*, I had payslips and could get a policy. This was a blessing, as had I not been covered, I would have risked all of my earnings for the show and more. It is thanks to Jeanne who insisted I take out cover, whether I could eat or not.

I spent two months in recovery, going to therapy sessions and bonding with my mum and family. Around May that year, *Strictly* had called again and I was asked to return for another season. This time they had secured a partner for me – I would be in the running as a professional on the main competition stage. It felt like the first time all over again; the thrill had lost none of its shine.

Chapter Eleven

Becoming Jojo

I left for the UK with a spring in my step. This time I understood the lie of the land. Going back, I could now afford my own apartment in Wembley, on the fourteenth floor – I wasn't going to risk letting those little furry monsters crawl up to my flat. I was firm in my conviction that the higher up I went, the safer I would be. I had also grown accustomed to the public transport in London, my mind accepting the need to squeeze in with other commuters. After my first year, I had also adapted to the gruelling switch from Britain's faltering summertime to the unforgiving autumn and winter. It was endlessly gloomy, with very little sunshine, if any. There were days in that first year when I'd be so cold that I'd actually start to feel depressed, just from my body's shock response to the temperature and lack of sunshine.

For the first couple of days, I would sleep late into the morning, engulfing myself in warm blankets. That was until I learned that the trick was to wake up as early as 7am and soak in whatever flicker of sunshine there was to be had. Having spent most of my life in sunny South Africa and tropical islands during my years on the ships, there was no denying that I thrived on sunlight. When the sun peered out from the clouds, it was like welcoming an old friend back into my life. Coming back this time, I was prepared for anything: weather, transportation and more. What I could never have anticipated was the sensation that *Strictly*'s first same-sex dance would spark.

The best thing about my return was that I was about to live on my own for the first time. For my whole adult life, I had lived out of a suitcase and shared with housemates or cabinmates. From thirteen, when I moved in with the Palemans, I had been a rolling stone. Now, for the first time, I could afford to buy my own set of pots, a bed of my choosing, sheets, cutlery and my very own microwave. I would be in IKEA on the phone with Mum, asking for tips on what I needed for the house. I was revived by indulging my favourite hobbies – cooking and baking. I took great comfort in the ritual of cooking. During my time on cruise ships, we had been all over the world and forced to eat whatever was available. But that meant that I was not afraid of trying to cook other cuisines, like Indian food. I would turn on the music and spend hours perfecting my kormas and biryanis, accompanied by a glass of wine. I loved to revert to food from Africa, like fufu, which is a dough made from boiled and pounded starch root vegetables like plantain and yam.

At *Strictly*, I was partnered with actress and implausibly amazing human being Catherine Tyldesley. Having competed before, I had determined that the two qualities I valued most in a partner were kindness and hard work. In Catherine, I found more than that.

From our first meeting, we hit it off, connecting instantly. Catherine and I were voted off on week six of the show, and I was sad to leave so soon, as I was enjoying dancing and spending time with her. It's terrible to be voted off after a process that brings two people together, and, for weeks, they create magical moments in rehearsals and in front of the cameras. It is a moment that is sacred to us because, even though millions watch, only the two of us are in that moment. To be told that it's the end feels like a death of sorts. It's like the ending of a good story when you are still relishing the journey. You can remain friends and you can meet up for coffee, but it is a new and different journey altogether. To wake up and see each other every day for weeks, all while facing the challenge of that week's dance, bonds couples in a unique way. By week three of sharing the journey, you can feel like you have had three years of being in each other's worlds – a function of how intensely and meticulously the *Strictly* magic works.

For those weeks, you have teams of people dedicated to ensuring that you put your best foot forward. From support choreographers, make-up, hair and creative direction, it's all geared to you. These people become part of your bubble as you dive head-first into the creative process. It's sad to go as it can feel like you are having a public break-up with the world watching as you are told it is the end of the line.

Along with the low of walking away on week six of that season, my second round of *Strictly* was also a year that prepared me for some major personal and professional milestones. The season was packed with lots of exciting musical acts, my favourite of which was a performance with one of the finest musical talents of her generation, Emeli Sandé. This was also the season I was asked to be part of *Strictly*'s first same-sex dance with my dear friend, Graziano. Alongside Luba and Aljaž, Graziano and I danced our hearts out to Emeli Sandé's 'Shine', as she stood behind us singing some of the most affecting lyrics about loving whoever you want and love shining through.

I was beyond pleased to see the direction that the show was taking. At the beginning of every season, the cast would sit around the table with the producers, choreographers and creative team to share ideas and plans for the latest iteration of the show. By co-creating with us, the producers brought us in on the big decisions in a truly collaborative way.

I loved that the subject of a same-sex number and bringing queer representation to the show was a direction about which the production felt strongly. Graziano and I were the best of friends. I imagine when they were thinking of which two men to pair, they thought of me for obvious reasons and him because who else did Johannes get on with better than Graziano? And so it was a done deal – we were going to be the first same-sex dance couple performing to a music act on *Strictly*. I couldn't have been more chuffed to have been partnered with my incredible friend and talent.

At that point, the significance of the moment had yet to sink in, and I hadn't begun to consider what that dance might mean for the show's audiences. It felt like just another day at work. Perhaps it was because of the way in which the routine was so carefully put together. It was emotive and moving, with stunning choreography.

I remember how confident I felt stepping onto the *Strictly* stage for that history-making dance. It was so carefully packaged and expressed, easing our audiences into the story of love and how it comes in a rainbow of hues. I thoroughly enjoyed dancing with Luba, Aljaž and Graziano, with Emeli Sandé right there, sharing the dreamlike moment with us. I relished every second.

I'll never forget the response to the dance, with one viewer saying: 'Thank you to these two courageous young men for doing such a thing.'

In just a few minutes of TV gold, we had set in motion a whole debate. Along with the good, also came some complaints. I sincerely wish there was a way to read the good without seeing the bad. Some people were threatening to stop watching the show if that was the direction in which the production was heading. I was more than a little bit devastated to see a number of messages from women expressing their disappointment that I had chosen to embrace same-sex dancing. For them, I had let them down. I was deeply affected by these tweets for a time. In these women's faces, I saw my own mother and aunts. It took me time to recompose myself and look past those homophobic remarks. As disturbing as I found them to be, I was undeterred – dance is my refuge, and nobody can touch me when it comes to that world.

Like dealing with my childhood bullies, I learned not to engage, avoiding opening the proverbial can of worms. I chose to 'pay the naysayers no mind' and to keep forging ahead. Forge ahead I did until an episode so visceral it turned my world inside out – the moment my most private dreams played out to the world. My past and present were colliding. After the thirty-two years Johannes had spent hiding in plain sight, Jojo was born, wearing his heart on his sleeve and bringing all of himself to bear.

After my performance with Graziano, I was asked to wear heels and pay homage to the 'vogue' underground dance movement. Talk about turning up the volume. From our tastefully executed routine with Emeli Sandé, I was now being asked to raise the temperature.

This time I would be standing solo, without another *Strictly* professional next to me. It would be me with heels on and an attitude fit for ten drag queens. The producers and choreographer, Elizabeth Honan, had pitched the idea to me during our pre-production and rehearsal period. They explained that for week five's group number, they would be presenting the cast as stars at the Met Gala. I was to strut the red carpet in heels, complete with a whacking and voguing routine with two back-up dancers. The idea would be executed elegantly, with respect to the community and culture.

I instantly recognised that this was my moment to definitively declare my sexuality. If you didn't know before, you would by the end of my performance. When you are a six-foot-two man in a pair of heels with bold make-up on one of British TV's biggest shows, you cannot hide behind an illusion of silence. This would be my official coming out to the world party.

Before our studio recording, I had multiple fittings with the wardrobe team to find me the perfect heels. The exceptional wardrobe team borrowed the famous long red boots from *Kinky Boots The Musical*. I was honoured to step into those shoes but quickly realised that they were too high for me. They were six inches tall, and I needed to do dips, turns and struts. So in a flourish of true small-screen sorcery, they created special two-and-a-half-inch leather ankle-length boots with laces, especially for me.

From the moment I put them on, I was buzzing. It reminded me of the days I spent as a child in Ausi Mpho's shoes. Mum's openness to my infatuation with women's shoes made it all the more confounding that she did not stand up for me when my uncles would badger me about when I would bring home a wife. During one of my visits home during my years on the ships, I fell out with Mum on the issue. It was neither the first nor last time my uncles had chastised me about the existence of a wife or girlfriend – but it was the first time that I had lost it with Mum.

We were at a family funeral when my uncles had probed, once again, my efforts to get a girlfriend. One went as far as asking if I needed some assistance and whether he should organise me one, as I clearly seemed to be struggling to meet women. I lost it that day.

'What? You want to organise what, and for who?' I fired back before giving my mother a death stare and walking away.

I had never had the confidence to say: 'Never going to happen Bob.'

Still furious, I was disappointed with myself for not disclosing my truth. Instead, I took it all out on my poor mum. I challenged her silence, demanding to know why she didn't say anything to her brothers when they were harassing me. Mum sat there quietly. Then the words flew out of my mouth before I could catch them.

I said, 'You do know that I am gay, right?

Still, my mother did not respond. I knew full well that my mother did not like confrontations. The fact that I was enraged would not get us anywhere. It was the first and last time that I ever uttered those words to her. We never spoke about it again. We drove back home quietly in the car. Deep down, I understood that my mum was not the enemy. In that moment, I just needed to let off some steam. My loving mum, who had always avoided conflict, allowed me the room to get this issue off my chest.

For most of my life, I have struggled with feeling like I was a fraud because of instances when I did not have the willpower to stand up to people like my uncles, or my bullies when I was younger. I have often heard accomplished stars talk about imposter syndrome. And while I have not personally struggled with imposter syndrome around my work, I have silently suffered with the shame and guilt of not being able to feel fully at home in my own skin. I would often ask myself, who am I? How could I have the courage to show up as myself – even in front of my macho uncles? The trauma of growing up exposed to bullying and being punished for who I was ate away at me. All the emotional blows I had endured had left an internal wound that had been festering under the surface.

One of the many memories I had buried was of my friend Jeff being beaten up for playing with Barbie dolls and make-up with me when we were kids. I found this inexplicable because my family had created a safe haven for me and my friends. We were allowed to play with heels and dolls and to paint our nails. But Jeff had been beaten black and blue. He was so badly hurt that he didn't come to school the next day. A day that had started so ordinarily, with the three musketeers innocently playing together, would end with such violence. I couldn't wrap my head around Jeff being hurt purely for being gay.

For many, coming out is an ordeal. Even when we learn to create safety among ourselves, when we step out into the world, or sometimes within our very own homes, we are up against unknown threats.

I knew that even after blurting out my sexual orientation to my mum back in my early twenties, it was not 'formally' coming out. Coming out can happen over many years and, for me, is an ongoing experience. Even when you are as camp as Christmas like me, the world still demanded that I make my position known, or else the questions about a wife and kids would keep coming.

As part of my preparation for the boys in heels dance, I threw myself back into episodes of *Pose*. Rewatching the show helped me to understand the complex nature of internalised shame, as well as the twin fights for acceptance and against prejudice. I stepped back and realised that, after all these years, there was still a need for better representation. Although the show is set in the eighties, the reality is not very different today. There are still so many members of the LGBTQIA+ community who remain oppressed, in danger and having to hide their true identity. As I looked at the cast on *Pose*, I realised how underrepresented we are on mainstream television. A show like *Pose* was special because trans people were well-represented. As the drama unfolded, I saw parts of myself in the stories being told. The show gave me a sense of empowerment that I needed to step inside those heels. I donned them knowing that I was not alone, that I was but a small part of a beautiful community. The true step change was that, for the first time, I would not have to hide or imagine myself as my mother or Ausi Mpho; I could step inside my own heels as Jojo, and not an imagined persona.

Once I had done some mental preparation, I became obsessed with the art of voguing and whacking. I came from a Latin and ballroom world, so voguing had not been a style that I was well-versed in. If I was going to step on that stage to represent this very important cultural moment, I wanted to do it justice. Fortunately, *Strictly* was two steps ahead of me as usual. They had organised sessions with a voguing and whacking specialist to put me through my paces. We worked on my section and workshopped it to perfection. We were not about to take chances and there was a shared commitment to go all the way. And crucially, nothing is left to chance.

As we edged closer and closer to the recording, I started feeling more at one with the moment. I understood that maybe it would be fleeting and not affect anyone, but it felt huge. For me, it was monumental.

I had been told so many times before that I needed to tone it down. One time in South Africa, someone reminded me to tone it down because the women who were voting cared about how I came across. Throughout my life, I had been repeatedly told that I was 'too much'. Here was a moment where I was told to let loose, to put on the heels and strut on a global stage. To not dim my light.

After learning the group sections with everyone, it was time to run the whole thing in rehearsals. From the moment my section came in, my *Strictly* family lost it. The first cheers I got were from my lovely castmates and the production team. When we filmed the final production number, it felt like our entire production team had come on set to bear witness. There was electricity in the air. Our colleagues from all departments wanted to see the number. It would be the first time boys in heels would be featured on the BBC's *Strictly Come Dancing*, during a prime-time slot. The anticipation was palpable.

From the second the *Strictly* band kicked off David Bowie's 'Fame' to a jam-packed, expectant studio and we all dropped on stage one at a time, my nerves began to dissipate. I felt the old me leave my body as I swung my hips side to side, filled with determination and fire. All the while, I said to myself: 'This is for every Black man, or gay man, or woman who's ever felt like a misfit, inadequate or different. You show up and show up for yourself.'

After the show, I packed my bags and went home. I woke up the next morning to a flood of calls and countless messages on my social media. My phone rang all morning, and I received thousands of messages from people thanking me on Twitter and Instagram. I had youngsters calling me an icon.

'Nobody has ever come on and owned their sh** the way you just did on that floor,' read one.

My mind was blown. I had decided to use that moment to own my truth, and I was received with more compassion and positivity than I could ever have wished for.

This was also the moment I was sure that Britain was a place I could call home. For most of my life, my relationships with men had been about being loved in secret or shrouded in shame. Over time, that can make you feel unworthy of being loved openly. The flood of positive affirmations and messages of love that I received after that dance helped me on my healing journey. Learning to love myself wholly. Learning that I was worthy of love. This was my new chapter.

Saying yes to those heels was my answer to everyone who had ever made me question and doubt myself. It was a proud moment where I declared that never again would I apologise for who I am. That show reminded me that there had been nothing wrong with me all this time. From the immediate feedback of our studio audience, who responded with a standing ovation, to feedback from viewers at home, I felt love and adoration like I'd never felt before for owning my truth that way. Stepping into those heels felt like home to me. In that moment, seven-year-old

Johannes and thirty-two-year-old Jojo hugged and made peace. No more toning it down to please others; no more blurring into the background.

After that show, people would stop to ask where I had learned to walk in those heels. I would nod to little Johannes, who wasn't always brave enough to own his mastery. I had learned the secret of walking in heels as a child, already seeing the superpowers that they could give you. Any person who has felt at home inside a pair of heels will tell you that there is an instant sense of power and poise that you feel from the moment you slide your foot inside. You know that you mean business. Whether you are going to a meeting, running errands or owning your sexy, heels not only elevate you but shift the way you carry yourself.

When I wear heels, I can feel my inner Naomi Campbell emerge. It is for this reason that I have quietly envied my mum. On the rare occasions that she would doll herself up, she would throw on her high heels and, in those moments, I wanted to be her. It was the way she carried herself and how her persona changed every time she wore those Pierre Cardin heels. It was my first lesson in the art of transformation and was a liberating thing to witness.

I wrapped up my second season feeling transformed and with more self-appreciation than I ever thought possible. The year came to a glorious end as Oti won the glitterball.

After the show wrapped, my aunt summoned me home again for what would be our final Christmas with her, and the last festive period before all of our lives were turned upside down by Covid-19. I arrived home from England on 17 December 2019 and stayed three weeks. Mum and Auntie Martha's eldest sister had passed away, but due to work, I had not been able to make the funeral. After all our traditional rituals had been observed and having spent some time with my family over Christmas, I flew back to England for the *Strictly* tour rehearsals. Catherine sadly suffered an injury halfway through the tour that year. This meant that, for half of the tour, I had mostly group numbers, as my partner was down. After the tour ended towards the end of February, I decided to return home and see family again. Without the *Burn the Floor* tour that year, I had enough time to see my family before our *Strictly* run later that year.

Then, in March, the world went into lockdown as the pandemic struck with a vengeance. I thanked God that I was lucky enough to be stuck at home with my mum and loved ones. There was a lockdown in South Africa, but, where I was, you could not stay in your house and expect to eat. People didn't have saving accounts and grocery delivery or click-and-collect services. I'm not sure how our government ever expected us to function while staying in our homes.

I prayed that the pandemic would pass as quickly as possible so that we could all return to work. There was fear on so many levels, not just about health but about what would happen with my career. I had finally got to this amazing place, and the world was turned upside down.

Strictly usually called around May to confirm our contracts, but, that year, we waited until June. There was so much at stake, and they were working tirelessly to weigh the feasibility of running the show amid strict regulations and a rampaging epidemic.

Like many people who feared for their livelihoods in those first difficult months, I was anxious about work and for everyone who depended on the show for their income. I also considered our loyal fans and how *Strictly* was their companion during the winter months. Eventually, the team and I worked to ensure that I could get special exemption to fly back to England from South Africa to work on the show.

My work permit was fortunately approved, and I was able to return in time to join the crew at The Manor hotel in Aylesbury.

We were to stay at the hotel for a full month and get into our rehearsals and pre-shoot a chunk of our group numbers. The entire month of August that year was dedicated to group performances. We all had to be extra careful and remain in a bubble with our partners. Essentially our partners were the only people we could touch and mix with for most of the time. One person being infected could jeopardise the entire production, so the stakes were high. We all understood why we had to be on board, and everyone wanted to make the show work. For a time, we weren't even sure if the show would be able to go into production that year. Now that we were so far in, none of us wanted to throw it all away. We were happy to make small personal sacrifices and compromises to bring a little bit of joy to people during one of the most trying periods in history. We all felt a sense of duty.

Seeing the likes of my partner Caroline Quentin, a national treasure in the UK, selflessly leave her house to do the show at a time when it was safer to be home was nothing short of inspiring. Caroline is an award-winning comedian, actress and television presenter whom I found truly witty and caring. I was astonished when I was told I was being entrusted with her. She's a dame and a veteran of the industry and is well-regarded for her expertise and journey. We had a wonderful run on the show together, even though we were voted off in week five of an unusually nine-episode season. Surprisingly, Mum said she had foreseen our exit that week. We had done our cha-cha-cha, and we had a wonderful time gliding across the stage for our final dance. Week five was not a bad outcome as, due to Covid, there were only a few more episodes before the finale. I somehow understood, accepting gracefully that it was our time to go home. I left the show to discover that I would not be able to join my family for Christmas that year. Going back home to South Africa was not advisable at that point after the discovery of a new strain of Covid in South Africa. I would be missing our family gathering, which had grown ever larger over the years. It threw my distance from my friends and family into sharp relief, leaving me feeling isolated and alone.

Chapter Twelve

And Just Like That . . .
Her Job Here Was Done

The phone rang and it was my cousin with dreadful news. It was 13 February 2021 and they were asking if I had heard the news about Aunt Martha.

'What news?' I snapped back.

'Umm . . . Someone said something, but it's not confirmed . . . let me call you right back,' he stuttered as he hung up before I could get in another word.

I frantically dialled my mum.

'Why didn't you tell me about Auntie Martha?' I asked accusatorially.

'What about her? Last time I heard, she was still in hospital. What did you hear?' Mum said.

Silence fell as we both struggled to choose the next words. My pulse was racing as I realised that something was wrong.

'Baba, let me call you back,' she urged, leaving me hanging as she abruptly hung up.

She called my uncle, who had been on the line with her a few minutes before I had rung her. Knowing how close my mum and Aunt Martha were, my uncle had wanted to break the news to her as gently as possible, so he had asked if she could meet him at the family home. My mum had apparently told my uncle that she was not coming to the house that day because her sister was coming back home. My uncle sensed that my mum was in denial about what had just happened, so told her to stay put and that he would go to her.

We all knew that Aunt Martha had been in the hospital longer than usual this time around. She had long suffered from diabetes, and a coronavirus infection had left her gravely ill. In South Africa, as in many parts of the world, Covid-19 patients weren't allowed visitors, leaving the hospital to update us by phone. The family had been praying for her quick recovery and remained hopeful as we knew Aunt Martha was a fighter who could defeat anything.

From my cousin's call, I had a nagging feeling that something was wrong. I could feel it inside of me. I felt the ground shift under me, a seismic shift. Those few minutes before Mum rang back were some of the worst moments of my life. After receiving my call, Mum phoned her brother and demanded to know exactly what was going on with Martha. I was struggling to breathe in Wembley, alone in my apartment in the middle of winter. By the time Mum stopped crying enough to call me back to confirm my worst fears that Aunt Martha had died, I was sitting on the floor in my apartment, tears streaming down my face uncontrollably. I knew there would be no need to dry them, so I just let them continue until my T-shirt was soaking wet.

After that call with Mum, I endured my first anxiety attack. My heart was beating fast as I lay on the floor of my apartment for hours, struggling to breathe or move. I wondered whether I was having a heart attack and would die too. The fear was raw and unrelenting.

Aunt Martha's passing dredged up memories of every other death in my family, losses I had sought to bury. I had lost my maternal grandmother and grandfather, as well as aunts and uncles, in the years that I was away working. From a family of ten siblings on my mum's side, there were now only three left after Aunt Martha's passing. I had missed all of those funerals. I had always had to grieve by myself, either on a ship or on tour somewhere far away. I had mourned each passing with great sorrow, away from the comforting embrace of loved ones, but somehow I had always managed to pull myself together. Aunt Martha's death tore me apart. She had been such an important role model to me in my earlier years, and I loved her so much.

I was in Britain and could not go home for Aunt Martha's funeral. Covid-19 travel bans prohibited international travel, meaning I couldn't make the journey to South Africa. I had also just received my global talent visa at last, and my agent had booked me a string of jobs before the next season of *Strictly* was due to resume. I couldn't believe that my visa had finally arrived. In January 2021, Aunt Martha and I had spoken at length about me getting it, only for her to pass away a month later. I was broken.

Dragging myself out of bed and into the shower on the morning of my aunt's funeral was the most testing ordeal of my life. Knowing that she would have expected nothing less, I pulled myself together, washed and dressed in my best black suit and formal shoes. I sat in front of my laptop and watched my aunt's funeral virtually. Sitting through the service was gut-wrenching. To hear the cries of my family while I was miles away and unable to comfort them was agony. My heart broke for my cousins, who had lost their mum, and for my mum, who had lost her beloved sister and confidante. I would have given anything to be with my family at that moment.

Watching her colleagues dressed in their white nursing uniforms, I couldn't help but think they resembled angels. I broke down as I heard story after story about how my aunt went above and beyond to meet her patients' needs. One speaker recounted how my aunt had touched so many lives and influenced so many of her colleagues to grow within the profession. She cared deeply about people. In the midst of my deep sorrow, I felt grateful and proud to have had Martha as my aunt. I think you never fully understand the impact someone had when they were alive until they are gone. We felt her presence every day. She wore her heart on her sleeve and was always there for those she loved.

Two days after Aunt Martha's funeral, I had to pick myself up and face the world again. I was booked to start filming *Celebrity Masterchef*, where I was to take part in various cooking challenges under the watchful eyes of professional chefs. It is a very popular show and was in its sixteenth series, and I was happy to be asked, even if I was a little nervous. I spent time over lockdown practising in the kitchen, and I knew that I could make something palatable, and it was a challenge. In the end, I made it to the quarter-finals and was sent packing over a burrito. I didn't expect to be quite so gutted when I left. I gave a twirl as I was eliminated from the show, which received applause all around from my fellow contestants and the judges.

Over the years, I have learned to compartmentalise my feelings. I was a professional and put my feelings to one side. I was always able to do this to some degree, but however hard I jammed my feelings down during the day, I got home that night to find a flood of emotions still waiting for me to deal with.

While I did a passable job in the studio, and it was a beautiful distraction, I was battling guilt and an insurmountable amount of grief when I was alone with my thoughts. I begrudged myself for neglecting my family. I had missed too many weddings, birthdays, funerals, thanksgiving ceremonies and graduations to count. It was all too much. The pain of working hard to provide was compounded by missing life's special moments.

For a split second, I considered packing up my life and returning home to make up for the lost years, but realised that Aunt Martha would have not wanted that for me. She had always supported my aspirations. The best way to honour her memory would be to continue rising up and soaring. For the rest of that year, I worked myself to the bone.

Grief is a slow-burn emotion. It seeped deep into my core, and I found it capable of camouflaging itself against everyday life until it reared its head again. It hit me so hard that I didn't come out of my flat for three weeks. Curtains drawn, I shut myself off from the world, not eating, spending the entire time drowning in tears and sorrow. I cried and couldn't eat for close to three weeks. I lost the will to live. I had never had an episode like that in my entire life – tremendous pain that wore on me emotionally and psychologically. I kept in close contact with my family, and thank goodness for technology in that regard. I was not okay, and I think they sensed this. My people would never allow me to wallow in my pain and chatting to them helped, but I knew it was not enough. I worried that my family could never start to comprehend the life that I was living. It was like I was living in two worlds: Jojo in the township with the family and friends and this new world on TV. That disconnect was so apparent then more than ever. I was starting to be approached more frequently for different opportunities.

It was then that I realised it was time to seek professional help. In the midst of that darkness, I finally had to admit to myself that the pain was unbearable and I could not suppress it or distract myself with work. It occurred to me that if the pain I was enduring had been physical, I would have gone to accident and emergency without hesitation. Through therapy, I got the help that I needed to delve into some of my grief and to do some much-needed work on myself.

I continued to balance therapy and work until it was time to return to *Strictly* rehearsals. Covid-19 still had its claws out as countries all over the world battled to vaccinate their citizens. To limit the risk of infections, the cast and crew had to lodge at The Manor again for the rehearsal run. By this time, I was in a much better place. *Strictly* had always been a happy place for me. I was delighted to return to something that brought me joy, and I felt ready to get back on the dance floor.

We were called for our usual production briefing to plan the season ahead. It was at this meeting that the plan to cast a same-sex male couple was put forward. In the previous season, the show had successfully introduced its first female pair, the incredible Nicola Adams and Katya Jones. Another historic *Strictly* moment.

They asked the male professional dancers if we would be comfortable to be paired up with another male. They understood it was a big responsibility that would bring a lot of attention, and that teaching and partnering a male is not something that many of us had lots of experience in. I said no outright, not comfortable to step into that role. I had enough to deal with emotionally that year as it was. I said no for my own personal reasons. I had already raised the flag of representation high in the previous season, and I had done my bit. Now I needed to focus on my own healing and continue building on the work I was doing in therapy.

The truth is that, even though I had come a long way in accepting myself, I was still fearful. All of those stored memories of being bullied and trolled online had not just evaporated. Therapy had helped me to see that it's possible to forgive and begin to let go of the pain, but it's hard to completely forget. Those memories stay with us, just as good memories are imprinted in our minds, and can take a while to work through. I felt self-protective and didn't feel like putting myself in such a vulnerable position at that stage in my life. I spoke about it to some of my closest friends and confidants, but not Mum. Where I come from, we don't talk about such things. There's an unspoken rule within my mum's generation that they can respect you as a person, but to sit down and have a lengthy conversation about matters of sexuality was taboo. So, I held back. I wasn't ready for this.

One of the best things I did was to accept a sit-down invitation with my *Strictly* boss Sarah James, who had been promoted to the position of executive producer the year I was returning for the second time. She and I had forged a bond during her days as the show's producer. We first met in South Africa while I was shooting *Dancing with the Stars* there, and I took an immediate liking to her.

Sarah, whom I held in high regard and trusted implicitly, helped me to understand that *Strictly* was on a journey to bring its audiences along with the exciting new developments. The show was taking a stand on how it wanted to look and feel as it moved forward. She stressed the work I had done through high-profile routines, and my outspokenness about owning my sexuality meant I was uniquely placed to help the show achieve the inclusivity and diversity it stood for and wanted to champion. She helped me realise that it would be a missed opportunity for me not to be part of that breakthrough. After I shared my fears about my safety, in the event of a backlash, she assured me that the production would go to great lengths to protect me. It was exactly what I needed to hear, but I told her that I needed to think about it one last time.

I went home and soon came to the realisation that I was the only person standing in my way. I came to see that whether I accepted that opportunity or not, people were still going to have their opinions. I needed to filter out other people from my decision-making and concentrate on my own peace of mind. Once I simplified it, I didn't need to dig deep for courage. This was a dream come true, and I was not about to self-sabotage to placate bullies and online trolls. I had friends like Oti, my agent Antony and cousin Teddy cheering me on.

'It's about to go down,' I said presciently, making the decision to go ahead.

Not a lot of people would understand how personal and healing that step might be for me. I begged them to will this opportunity for me and walk with me through it.

After deciding to do it, I called Sarah and told her I would be honoured to have the opportunity to step into that role. I had gone the full 180 degrees. From doubt to wanting this so badly, I was tearing up. It was like an awakening that had spurred me on. It had never crossed my mind that ballroom and Latin American dance would ever get to this place in my lifetime. Here was the moment, practically being handed to me. It would be impossible for me to say no to it.

This was the stuff my childhood dreams were made of. It was about to be realised in full technicolour. And I was there for it.

After the initial flurry of exchanges and the excitement of agreeing to do it, there was a long wait. None of the dancers are ever told in advance who their partners are going to be for the season until the day on which the reveal is being taped. Part of the show's integrity is making sure everyone's reactions to the season's partnering are utterly authentic. That moment, which is captured by cameras all around, is as real for the viewers as it is for us. The day was filled with anticipation. All I was told was that we would be driving north to meet my partner.

I was well aware that there were a few personalities joining the show that year who lived in the north of England, and John Whaite was one of them. I was hoping that it would be his house we were driving to. We arrived at this gorgeous farmhouse in his hometown. Once we had parked up, one of the producers told me that the plan was to have me jump out of a giant cake for the reveal. It was then that I knew it was him.

There was only one celebrity baker on the show.

Now I knew without a doubt that it was John, I felt a hint of nerves that belied my excitement. It was a feeling I had never had in all my years on *Strictly*. That's not to take anything away from any of my wonderful previous partners from years past, but this just felt different. All my life I had mastered the dance between a man and a woman, and now I was about to walk into a world I had not spent years preparing for.

I cha-cha-cha-ed inside the cake and was wheeled into position. On cue, I popped out of the cake and there he was, the man with whom I was about to make history. He was handsome and tall, with a smile that affirmed we were going to get along. He was likeable and appeared polite and friendly. I felt my nerves giving way to euphoria.

Here was a man who was unapologetic about his life. He was gay and proudly out. He was clear about his intentions from the very first day of our meeting. He guaranteed me that he would work hard, and it was in that moment that I realised I had been paired with someone who matched me in strength. As soon as we started chatting, I realised how many similarities we shared. I felt right away that it was going to be a harmonious season. I could set aside any fears of a personality clash.

John and I were about to embark on the rollercoaster ride of our lives. Once the chit-chatting was done, it was down to the dance, a challenge that would dominate our lives for fourteen weeks straight.

For the first time, I walked into *Strictly* feeling the weight of not just being the choreographer and teacher, but also of being the student. This was my first experience learning to dance in such a pairing. I had certainly never before partnered with another male. I had no references or templates on which to draw. Creatively, I was stretched. Emotionally and physically, I had to grow in leaps and bounds.

The subtleties are different in a male–male pairing. It's not the same as having the confidence of being coupled with a female partner and knowing my place as the party that leads. Here was a man who I needed to teach how to lead, as well as be led at the same time. We both needed to learn how to be the picture and the frame, when all my life I had been the frame. To strike that balance with the eyes of the world watching us in the limited time we were given took great skill and nerves of steel, qualities for which I will always respect John. It took us a couple of weeks to gel, but when we did, it felt like magic.

Like everyone, I think my mum waited to see how it would play out because she's such a traditionalist. I remember our first tango – she called me: 'Oh, that was brilliant,' she said. Those words felt special.

For fourteen weeks straight, I hardly slept. I have terrible insomnia when I am stressed. The pressure was not letting up. Just as we nailed that week's performance on a Saturday, I would go home and already start working on our next dance and prepare our rehearsal plan for the following Monday. This meant that my Sundays, which were supposed to be my rest days, were essentially occupied with choreographing, and conceptualising that week's choreography. Due to the glare of the spotlight on us, I felt intense pressure to present something hard-hitting every week. We couldn't let the world down – not with so many people cheering us on. This was both a blessing and a curse. The stakes were heightened from the outset when John and I took to the stage to perform the tango in the first week. I had internally expected that we would not live to see episode four. I did not expect the public to warm to this big, queer and interracial coupling and carry us to the finale. I had been in the show long enough to know that, at the end of the day, it all boiled down to the votes. We could dance our hearts out, but the final call was theirs. They could either vote in order to keep us in the show or not vote – which would put us at risk of having to face the ghastly elimination. To my surprise, we smashed expectations and, for my first time on the UK show, I made it to second place on the leader board. Rave reviews came in from viewers, press and stars alike. One tweet in particular from beloved television host and author Richard Osman to his million-plus followers struck our heartstrings at *Strictly*: 'And that's how you change the world for the better #Strictly,' he wrote.

Our dancing was covered in every paper in the country, and people were talking about our partnership.

Even as we basked in this special moment, it was clear there was work to be done with small pockets of society. We had made some progress, but the battle was clearly far from over. The swirling media storm from that season risked distracting me from the task at hand, so I got off social media for my sanity and to preserve what energy I had left for the dance floor. I was encouraged that our supporters far outweighed the trolls, but I still needed to ignore the naysayers like I ignored the bullies in my childhood. I did know that we had thousands of people reaching out through various platforms to express their support and encouragement, and I was encouraged by this. Hundreds of thousands of people said 'yes' through their votes week in and week out.

John and I were clear in our intentions from the outset that we wanted to win on merit and not because of public sympathy. It had to be about the dance. The process of allowing myself to focus on the thing that mattered most revealed to me a new kind of love for my art form. I discovered new ways of doing things and broadened my perspective of what dance could be as we broke through the ceiling of convention and old traditions. Through this partnership, I was learning to honour the old while discovering new ways of interpreting the language of ballroom and Latin.

John and I danced our hearts out week after week, right through to the finale episode. We won the audience's hearts with our rumba to Sting's 'Shape of My Heart', a *Pirates of the Caribbean*-themed paso doble and, my personal favourite, the Argentine tango to Beethoven's *Symphony No. 5* as reimagined by David Garrett.

For fourteen weeks, John and I explored every possible human emotion on the *Strictly* floor – from powerful, sensual, lustful, fighting and loving. We expressed a wide range of stories that reflected a shared universal human experience that transcended colour, gender, class or sexuality. It was an act of great joy and fulfilment every time we hit our mark, and that triumphant feeling carried us right through to our last count of every number. I cried every week without fail because of the empowerment and contentment every moment brought me. I was also filled with enormous gratitude for the audience who came along for the ride, lapping up every dance, again proving that dance knows no boundaries. We danced our way to the finale to be crowned as the runners-up as the brilliant Giovanni Pernice and Rose Ayling-Ellis lifted the glitterball, an honour of which we were both immensely proud. We were humbled to have had the beautiful people of the United Kingdom support us all the way to the finish line.

Even on the high of a truly successful season, I felt it was important to go home for Christmas that year. It would be our first Christmas without Aunt Martha, so a really difficult one to face. *Strictly* plays a week later in South Africa, so I was looking forward to our tradition of watching the show at her house together with the rest of the family. On Boxing Day morning, the family woke up, and it was agreed we would drive to Martha's grave so I could see where she had been laid to rest.

Standing there with a bouquet of flowers, surrounded by my family reopened the wound of that funeral day which I quickly understood had not healed for my family either. Some of us wept like it was the day of her funeral all over again. Later, I was thankful we were able to share this moment as it helped me to process my own grief. It was comforting to share in that process with my family and loved ones.

Later that day, when we sat down for lunch at Aunt Martha's house, the mood of sadness had begun to give way as we celebrated her memory and laughed, reminiscing about her and mimicking what she would be saying if she were still around. There can be great healing in this collective sharing of bereavement. We played some of her favourite tunes and my mum brought the house down when she got up and danced.

It was a miracle to see Mum move because she hardly ever did. It must have been years since I last saw her throw shapes like that, but when she does dance, it is a marvel to watch. Jocobeth Ramagole is, believe it or not, a splendid dancer.

That day she did not miss an opportunity to remind everybody that 'I got it from my mum'. I burned with pride and felt closer than ever to my family and ancestors than ever before.

It was a lovely day with so many family members coming to pay their respects. My uncles, aunties and cousins wanted to be sure that I was okay. They understood the pain we all suffered losing Aunt Martha. She was the foundation on which our family was built. I was deeply moved by their consideration and the love I felt. As I came to terms with the loss of one of my life's lodestars, I was nourished by the love I felt from my extended family. There had been this huge void from the day my auntie died. I felt deeply lost in the world without her and without my family to help me process the loss. The guilt of missing her funeral fell away, and with that I exhaled for the first time in an eternity.

After the season I had just had with John, I felt my family's turnout that day was a statement of their love and support. I had flown home with so many questions at the back of my mind. Would my uncle ask me what it was all about? What would my cousins say about me dancing with a man on a global TV show? I expected them to have a field day grilling me. Instead, there was no interrogation or mockery. There was nothing to address. Nothing to feel shameful about. I had carried all of this shame all of my life, and it appeared that most of my family didn't care and were too busy minding their own business and worrying about themselves to judge me, which I believe is a lesson to hold on to.

The highlight of my day was when the family congregated around the telly that night to watch the finale episode. My mum, Jabulile and cousin Teddy provided a running commentary. It was fantastic that, throughout my dance career, it had, above all, been my aunt who had championed my dancing. Now, in her absence, the rest of the family had finally caught on. I thought she must have been up there laughing. The cheering and commentary from the family's football fans were just as loud as they would have been for a match. It was hugely reassuring that she left just as my family were at last on board. It felt like such an Aunt Martha move.

It turns out that it would take that moment on *Strictly* for my uncle to stop asking about 'a wife and kids' and, most importantly, for me to feel unashamed about my sexuality. Throughout that season of *Strictly*, John and I had been so open about our sexuality that there was no wondering left to be done. If you watched even one episode of that season you would know that we were not only *Strictly*'s first same-sex competing male couple, but we were both gay. And, at last, I was free. The thought of bringing a boyfriend home was finally on the cards. I sat with that thought and let it percolate.

It was fascinating that we were gathered at Aunt Martha's house when she was the only person who would stand up to my uncles when they would badger me.

'What do you want to do with his wife? Why don't you focus on your own wives and leave this child alone?' she had once snapped at a prying uncle.

She knew how to give it.

From that day onwards, I carried myself differently around my family. I guess everything changed . . . My confidence was boosted to a level I had never imagined possible. Shortly after that day, I rocked my Louboutin boots and strutted to the nearest corner shop with my head held high. For the first time, I didn't feel the need to hide from or fear anyone in Zamdela.

The intention was not to turn heads, which I admit it did – I just wanted to be myself.

'My work here is done,' I imagined Martha saying, with a satisfied clap of her hands.

Chapter Thirteen

To Get Lost Is to Learn the Way

There is an African proverb that 'to get lost is to learn the way'. This wisdom has always resonated with me. I returned to the UK on 3 January 2022, feeling whole. I got into the city and went straight into rehearsals for the *Strictly* tour. The professional dancers had a week before the celebrity partners joined to assemble the big numbers. It was such a joyful occasion to see John again, having last seen him during the finals when we won second place. I missed him. One of the things John said to me upon reconnecting was that I seemed lighter, an observation I thought showed genuine intuition. I did feel as light as a feather. More than being an excellent dancer with whom I delighted in dancing, John was a caring and compassionate human and friend. These were some of the qualities that I absolutely adored about him. The rehearsal process for the tour can be a great deal of fun. There's certainly a lot to get through, but at the same time, it's the part of the season when the pressure eases and the cast is not competing. This allows breathing space to mingle and have fun on the floor without all that added pressure. It also offers the entire cast the rare opportunity to hang out, let our hair down and enjoy the journey together.

I was excited for John to experience the tour. It is a beautiful way to get to know the people who have supported you throughout the season. It was also an opportunity to bring our partnership to an end. I knew that the *Strictly* tour would be the perfect ship to take us on from a chapter from which we had derived great strength. I was mostly looking forward to John experiencing a more relaxed side of me. Throughout our competition time together, I was focused entirely on the work. He didn't get to always enjoy the fun Jojo, the light and bubbly one, far removed from the intensity and focus needed to compete. Without that anxiety of the show hanging over us, we had a chance to celebrate our dance partnership. It was bittersweet, as I silently wished that our journey of celebration could have been our entire season.

We opened the tour in Birmingham and, I will say it again, I will never get used to playing to an arena of 10,000 people. It doesn't matter how well-known you are, every performance is unique and a modern marvel. John and I opened the couples' section for the tour with the fans' favourite – our *Pirates of the Caribbean* paso doble dance. It was lovely to see the whole tour experience through his eyes. And *Strictly* knows how to run a tour. From the catering to the accommodation and the arenas with thousands of supporters screaming your name, every detail is carefully curated. You are made to feel like an absolute star. On those arena nights, every one of us felt like we had won the glitterball.

One of the icons of broadcasting in Manchester, Mark Radcliffe, famously said it is a city that thinks a table is for dancing on, and there we actually won the glitterball following the audience vote, held at each stage of the tour. Manchester is a city after my own heart.

As we lifted up the glitterball in an arena full of cheering fans, John and I embraced, and I felt hugely appreciative of our journey. That was mixed with excitement for what lay ahead for us individually. We had been through two blissful months on tour, during which I relished the opportunity to join him again for some of our favourite routines from the season.

One of my other highlights was the *Bridgerton*-inspired dance with Kai, a routine that brought me to tears every night. It had meant so much to so many viewers during the season, and it held the same level of meaning to me every time we stepped on a stage to perform it. To be able to celebrate that dance with the thousands of audience members we were performing it for energised me enormously, a feeling I will remember for the rest of my life. Every evening the performance would start off with dead silence in the arena as an introductory clip was shown. Standing by backstage and listening to the silence in the crowded arena, you could hear a pin drop as the audience waited in anticipation for the dance section to kick off. Then, lights up:

I stand at the top of a high-rise platform with the *Strictly* professionals waltzing on the floor. There is silence as I welcome everyone to the King's banquet. I slowly glide down the stairs as my subjects bow in honour of their sovereign. Shortly thereafter, Kai steps forward to join me in a duet. The silence subsides as the audience erupts into applause as we glide elegantly on the floor. The music crescendos, and the dance picks up pace.

Taylor Swift's 'Lover' and 'Love Story' instrumentals accompany us as we write our bit on the stars of history. It's a beautiful evening. Bridgerton has birthed a new king. He is Black, queer and dances like he is leaving everything on that floor. It is a story that, as a child, I would have given everything to see on my telly growing up. And to Abuti Ben, my first dance guide who once told me if I kept going back to the studio, one day I too could wear the magical tailcoat, I did it, Ben.

All I could hear was the loud screams and applause in the arena. It was magical and was such an emotional part of the show for me every night. The music was tremendously emotive, which didn't help this queen of tears. The dance, the lighting, the costumes – it all came together so cohesively. I couldn't help but weep at the fairy-tale feeling of it all. It carried such personal resonance for me. When I say that I feel seen in the United Kingdom, it is because of moments like this. To see the audience sharing that moment with me, accepting me and celebrating my journey with open arms and appreciating it as much as I did, meant the world to me. The last few days of the tour were quite emotional. It felt dreadful to say goodbye, yet all good things must come to an end.

I wrapped up the *Strictly* tour and didn't have time to fully process how that chapter was coming to a close, even as I was leaping into my next adventure. I was about to debut the first solo theatre tour of my life, and it was all about to happen in Britain. It felt like one of those moments when I needed someone to pinch me. I was going to headline my own show: *Freedom* by

Johannes Radebe. It had been a long time in the making. When I signed with my agent, one of the top five goals I agreed with them was a solo tour. Here it was, finally about to play out before my very eyes.

With only three weeks between the end of the *Strictly* tour and the launch of *Freedom*, I was virtually absorbed by producing the show. I had to oversee the conception, choreographing, costuming and casting of the show.

I pulled in a talented choreographer, Jess Ellen, to come in as an associate choreographer as well as reaching out to my South African choreographer friend, Liam Anthony, to join me in the process of putting it all together. It was challenging but equally thrilling to be calling all the shots. It was the opportunity of a lifetime to curate my own show, allowing me to share my culture and my story in my own words. Our opening night was set for Bridlington in Yorkshire.

My team adopted an unwavering focus and created the show in the face of some genuine difficulties. Just a few days before opening night, we had to let go of our costume designer and find a replacement. In my personal quest for perfectionism and at the height of the behind-the-scenes drama, I told my producers that we had to cancel the show and stormed out of the rehearsal.

I was staying in a beautiful apartment right on Bridlington seafront. Every time I felt frustrated, I would take a walk on the beach. I would scream, breathe and take a moment for myself before turning back. There were days when I could have thrown myself into the sea, so overwhelmed was I by the sense that things were not going to my plan. A lot of my ideas were not possible due to budget constraints, and I understand why this was, but it was hard to reconcile because the expectation was high from all angles. A lot of the stories and music that I wanted to tell were under copyright, and everything cost too much money. I felt like I had put myself on the line, and the stakes were too high.

My agent Antony and the team of producers came to me when I had cooled off and reminded me that we all wanted a fantastic show, but we also had a contractual obligation to adhere to. If we failed to deliver the show, we could be sued. They were right, of course, not to mention that people had already bought tickets to come and see the show. This preoccupied me far more than the threat of litigation. Letting down the people who had believed in me enough to buy tickets to come to the show would be heart-breaking. We had already sold out in most venues before the tour even started. Still, I was worried about putting out a product that I wasn't happy with. I felt all these people deserved a top-notch production. I understand that people had spent money on the show, and they deserved this. I reasoned as calmly as I could that I was far more worried about people being disappointed and being short-changed than having to put out a statement that we were cancelling. I considered everyone's points and asked for more time to gather my thoughts.

Once I had settled down, I acknowledged that the show was almost at the point where I was happy with the choreography. It was the issue of costumes that was haunting me. I walked outside and called Mum, and asked what she thought. More than anything, she gave me an outlet to vent. Then I called my cousin, Teddy, who had told me that if I was ever in doubt, I should call home for a reminder of who I am. Teddy listened to me lament my fears and anxieties and proceeded to remind me that I was a 'Mthimkhulu', our clan name, and there was nothing I could not do or get over. He said that I was an African child and there was nothing I could not face and defeat. He urged me to pull myself together and redouble my effort. I went back inside, and the team and I put our heads together to resolve the loose ends. I had a lovely cast of performers whom each brought their individuality and diverse range of skills to the show. Facing the hurdles of putting something that great together for the first time united us and allowed us to each take ownership of *Freedom*. I wanted the show to feel as much theirs as it was mine.

It dawned on me that this show was actually happening when the feathers were finally delivered before our opening night. I was sitting across from the theatre in a small café. When the van parked and out came a short man who pulled a huge rainbow-coloured feather backpack and headpiece out of the back of his white van, I knew the show must happen.

'Darling this is happening, regardless of what is ready and what isn't fully polished,' I thought to myself. The show must go on! What many don't know is that at the final dress rehearsal before the show that evening, we were still waiting for some of our costumes.

Despite all the nerves, it was a roaring success. I still couldn't wrap my head around the idea that people had actually bought tickets to come see the show. It was exhilarating, but it was also frightening. I prayed that what I was performing resonated with them. This was even more frightening because the work was so close to my heart. I was essentially playing out my life on stage in front of an audience. Would I be safe? My life had been marred with bullies and trolls. Was I putting myself in harm's way by putting it all front and centre on a live stage? Would I need security? The world is full of reckless people. I was also aware that I didn't have the *Strictly* team to hide behind. This time I was alone – there was no one to call.

For the first time, I would stand on the stage with a microphone in my hand and host the show. I took the audience on a journey of my story in my own words, drawing a picture of some of the moments that have shaped me, of who I was and how I became Jojo, and the little boy, Johannes. I had a neatly typed out script, but then I worried it didn't capture the essence of what I needed to share. So I put the script away and spoke from the heart, telling my story like I would to a friend. We had an incredible opening night, easily one of the highlights of my performing career. Admittedly, in true showbiz style, everything was dazzling upfront, but there was first-night chaos and lots of laughter behind the scenes.

Backstage, my agent and producers were helping dancers squeeze into costumes. There was a great deal of trial and error from a production perspective, but the audience had no idea. At that point, all I could do was have fun with the audience. We were ready to show up and razzle dazzle. The show went seamlessly and they gave us a standing ovation at the end.

Freedom was not only a fantastic project for me creatively, but also the cathartic beginning of recounting my story. I hope these words will carry that process forward. Our show in Bridlington would be one of the best nights on the tour. When I saw folks singing along to Miriam Makeba, Angélique Kidjo and Flavour's 'Sawa', I wondered how I had even considered cancelling the show in the first place. People were having the time of their lives along with us. I couldn't remember the last time I had had so much fun and felt so at home. We knew from that same show that we had something special in *Freedom*. It was evident that we were on a journey to bring sparkle, feathers and joy to people across the country. Word of mouth and our audience's bold support led us to sell out the show in every town we visited, including London's Peacock Theatre. It really struck me how things had come full circle – from my early days in London doing *Burn the Floor*, to now, debuting my own sell-out tour. So much had changed for me – it was a dream realised.

During the rest of the tour, I met so many wonderful people and not once felt like the show was work. I was humbled to encounter many kind characters during our meet-and-greets and to hear their most personal stories. On any given day, when I was feeling worn out or demotivated, I would meet spirit-lifting audience members. One girl, in particular, struck me, recounting a story about her father being gay and how he had passed away after my season with John. She told me how *Strictly*, through our partnership, had helped her father broach the subject of his homosexuality. She tearfully shared how the family had been estranged from her father for years because of their homophobia. But due to their shared love of *Strictly*, they reconciled and had a conversation that helped them bury the hatchet. She and I both cried as she told me that her father died peacefully, and at peace. She thanked me for being part of a show that she and her father both loved. I cried even more when she said her father would have loved to have been there that night.

Moments and stories like this always bring tears to my eyes. For years, I had doubted dance was my life's calling and had qualms about how sustainable and lucrative it could be. Instead, it has surpassed my wildest dreams. I couldn't believe the capacity it had to heal and bring people together. I was filled with gratitude for the art form and its power to touch and transform people's lives. I had never before seen it in that light. I had started dancing for my own enjoyment. Everything else – its reach, its transformative force and the positive impact it had on people's lives – was never on my radar. In dance, I had found a calling, the purpose of which was bigger than I could fathom. Dance is the greatest gift that has been bestowed upon me.

In Manchester, John and some of my *Strictly* castmates came to support me and had only positive things to say about the show. I could hear their excitement all the way from my dressing room. After two months on the road, our last show was scheduled to run in Canterbury, Kent. I will never forget the energy in that theatre. It was one of the biggest and loudest venues we performed in. I have no idea if it was because it was our last show, but something inside me knew I had to announce the next year's tour at that venue. The audience went wild with excitement, their response all the confirmation I needed to know that this was a creation of which I could be proud and continue to nurture.

I ended that tour on a high, particularly after learning that, after several attempts, my mum's visa to travel to England had been approved. I was sad that she had missed the tour, something we had worked tirelessly to get her to see, but I couldn't have been happier to know that she was finally going to see me in my new adopted home.

I returned to London to a string of invitations to some wonderful events. *Strictly* had been nominated for a BAFTA in two categories that year: Best Series and Media Moment of the Year. Clinching the Media Moment award for that year was Giovanni and the superb Rose for their golden moment on the show. We jumped out of our chairs when they collected the award. Rose and Giovanni had created one of the most affecting and memorable moments in television and certainly belonged in the *Strictly* Hall of Fame.

It was a pleasure to reunite with my *Strictly* family in such a relaxed setting, all of us dressed up and dolled up without the pressure of filming our show. It was lovely to see industry friends, acquaintances and artists whose work I admired. I even managed to thank Graham Norton for having me on his fabulous show as part of my *Freedom* press tour. I wore two top hats – one on top of the other – on his show; I love to play with the idea of what is seen as 'normal' and have fun with fashion. I also struggled to keep myself together while chatting with Channing

Tatum. Graham was delighted with the response to my appearance and invited me again the following year for my next tour.

2022 was packed with exciting events. The BAFTAs is truly magnificent. To have Julianne Moore sitting two rows away, and mingling with stars like *Sex Education*'s Ncuti Gatwa and one of my favourite artists Olly Alexander, was a dream. It is an all-round fantastic affair, and I was so thankful to be there.

Earlier in the year, I was invited to make a guest appearance on *RuPaul's Drag Race UK vs the World*. I had been watching the show since its inception in 2009 and was thrilled to be asked. My role was to help the queens get their choreography on point and in formation. What an honour!

I also made an appearance on *Loose Women* and then again on *Loose Men*, where I joined Vernon Kay, Roman Kemp and Mike Tindall in a special episode to mark Mental Health Awareness Week. I felt proud to be included in a group of men who are advocates for the importance of talking about how we feel. I had never really sat down and talked with other men about things that really matter; it was always with my girlfriends. It was interesting to hear about other men's experiences.

I have never found being in front of the camera any easier. English is not my first language, and sometimes I still struggle to land on the right words when I am trying to express myself clearly. I think Vernon could see right through me.

'Don't worry, I've got you,' he said just before we went on.

A few days later, Mum arrived at Heathrow Airport with my sister Jabulile. Having agreed that I would be at Heathrow to meet them off their flight at 5am, I woke up an hour after their arrival, my alarm having failed to go off. To make matters worse, my mum and sister, though warned to dress warm, had put on light jerseys and had not anticipated how cold London in May could be.

I had arranged for special assistance for them at the airport, which meant they were picked up from the plane door and escorted to immigration. By the time I got to the airport, they had been waiting for more than an hour. As I turned the corner, all I saw was Mum's long face. If she could slap me, she would have. I knew that it was obvious to her that I had overslept. I couldn't lie. I rushed over and hugged them both. Mum barely responded. I had not arranged a taxi for them as I wanted my face to be the first they saw on arrival. Now the plan had blown up in my face.

The next thing I knew, my sister was calling me out. She was careful not to draw attention by shouting, but she definitely let me have it. She was even more upset because the airport chaperone had had to wait with them the whole time. She felt like the poor man had better things to do with his time than watch over them while I was snoring. I profusely apologised to the gentleman, and we laughed as he wished me the best with the journey ahead, giving me a knowing wink.

We walked the short distance to the car, by which point Jabulile and I were already laughing and talking rubbish as usual.

As we drove through the endless ring roads around Heathrow, I asked my mum why she was angry. It was a preposterous question because I already knew the answer, but I threw it out there to yank her chain. Just like on our regular telephone calls, Mum doesn't know how to beat around the bush, saying the first thing that comes into her mind. Before I could apologise again for my tardiness, she interrupted.

'Because your sister,' she said before looking out of the window and pausing for dramatic effect, knowing full well I was gasping for more.

'What's happening?' I probed, rolling my eyes with disbelief and letting out a small chuckle because I knew my mum was about to dish the dirt on my sister.

'Let me tell you a story,' she said. 'Your sister couldn't go to the loo on the plane, and I had to accompany her – at her age.'

She paused again for effect.

'Why?' I played along.

'I don't know what Jabulile thought was going to happen to her life in that small cubicle,' Mum scoffed.

Apparently, Jabulile had asked Mum to repeatedly accompany her to the on-board lavatory, to which Mum had initially refused, complaining that it was too small for both of them to squeeze into. She had insisted that Mum could stand outside and watch from there, lest she fell from the aircraft, 35,000 feet above the sea. Jabulile refused to get up from her seat until Mum agreed to hold her hand through her worst fear, pestering her until she relented. I had never laughed so hard, the story keeping me in stitches until we got home. It was so typical of Mum and Jabu to be at each other's throats, an endearing reminder of home life.

We arrived at my place and the first thing Mum did was

inspect the house. After she had satisfied her curiosity, she pressed her lips together and nodded her head, smiling.

'It's good to see that your place is clean,' she said.

I did not tell her that I had hired a cleaner. While I am generally meticulous, Mum is much more particular than me.

As impressed as she appeared, Mum put down her bags and, in no time at all, she had a cloth in one hand and a bucket in the other, wiping things that appeared perfectly clean to a normal person. I knew that this meant that she was comfortable. My sister and I prepared breakfast before I asked Mum to come downstairs with me to look for a dress for our visit to Buckingham Palace the next day.

I had been asked to become an ambassador of the Duke of Edinburgh's Award scheme and deliver a keynote speech about my experience to encourage award holders to pursue their dreams. The fact that my mum was able to come with me due to the timing of her visit was incredible. We were so excited. Mum was elated about the prospect of a visit to the palace, as she is an avid follower of the Royal Family. I wore a classic pinstriped suit, which was linen. I got her a white Victoria Beckham two-piece. Over the years, she had made great sacrifices to put the needs of her children and grandchildren ahead of her own. I knew that she had a few prized outfits, and I felt strongly about giving her a chance to look the part and feel like the queen she had always been to me. As she confidently stepped out of the fitting room, her VB fitted like a glove on her tiny figure. I chimed in that she was now officially an English girl and ready to have tea with the Queen. We laughed, and I couldn't have been more overjoyed that Jabulile and Mum were finally here. We got back in time for lunch, and Jabu asked that we have a South African favourite called pap, a sort of porridge made from maize meal. Mum whipped it together with wors (a type of sausage) and tomato relish, making the flat smell like home in Zamdela. It was better than anything I had ever tasted.

We woke up the following morning brimming with excitement for our day ahead, by royal appointment. My agent Antony came to drive us to Buckingham Palace.

It was the first garden party after the pandemic to recognise the Gold Award winners. Going behind the heavily guarded, gold-tipped gates of Buckingham Palace was breathtaking. Mum was awed by the opulence we were seeing. The walls were high, the garden immaculate and everything seemed to be encrusted with real gold. Mum was utterly transfixed, a striking state in which to see her because very little impresses her.

She was only brought back to earth by the attention on us as we made our way inside. There were lots of people who wanted to stop and chat, not just with me but with Mum as well. I knew that Mum, who can be a bit of a recluse, doesn't speak to strangers often, and I could sense her getting overwhelmed.

The lovely people who were surrounding us wanted to say nice things and congratulate her on my accomplishments. It was all a bit too much attention for Jocobeth from Zamdela.

In South Africa, *Strictly* is only available with a special satellite subscription, which means it isn't as readily watchable as it is in the UK. This was the first time that my mum came to understand the scale of *Strictly* in Britain. Though she had heard me talk about it, it was different altogether to see its reach like that. Thankfully, Antony realised that Mum was getting flustered and took it upon himself to look after her, which was a massive help to me as I fretted about my upcoming speech.

Later on, I had to go inside alone to meet Prince Edward, who was hosting the garden party, and would join Antony and Mum outside in the garden after my speech. I bid farewell to both of them and followed the gentleman inside the palace. Then it hit me that I was about to meet the Earl of Wessex, and all I had was my speech. I panicked because I didn't feel prepared for how to handle myself around the prince. What was I going to say to the man when I met him in person? The last thing I wanted was to blurt out, 'Hi babe' in a moment of nerves. That would be a tabloid story to eclipse even Jabu's plane potty paralysis.

'Do I curtsy? Bow? Shake his hand? What do I do?' I asked the footman nervously. He calmly told me that the prince would extend his hand, and I could then shake it. He reassured me that the prince was a lovely man and that he would most likely do everything in his power to put me at ease. I was unsure if the pep talk had steadied my nerves. I was, however, grateful for his help.

Another participant and I were led into a room to meet the Earl of Wessex before we would go outside to give our speeches to the assembled guests.

The first thing the Earl of Wessex said to me was that his wife, the Countess of Wessex, would have been delighted to meet me and was envious that it was him meeting me, not her, as she loved the show and congratulated me on everything I was doing.

'He's human, Johannes. Calm down,' I told myself.

The prince was the picture of grace and poise. He effortlessly made all of us feel welcome and asked us each such insightful questions. At one point, he asked how I was finding life in the UK. He later introduced me to the 3,000-strong crowd with truly humbling comments about my work and journey.

As I stepped on stage to speak, I looked at my mum wrapped in a blanket and felt a rush of emotion. Ahead of my speech, I had overheard two valets discussing the Queen's blanket. One was asking the other where he was delivering it. There was a lady downstairs who was said to be freezing, his colleague answered.

'Mmm . . . that could only be my mother,' I chuckled to myself.

She had been griping about how cold it was before I even went up to speak. Antony must have clocked this and asked the staff to bring her something to keep her warm.

My voice was shaking as I took it all in and read my speech, but I was determined to push through because I had something to say. It was a powerful moment for me. As I addressed the young recipients of the award that day, I quietly spared a moment for little Johannes. Not long ago, he too was just as young and with so much to look forward to. I urged the young people listening in the garden to never doubt themselves. If I could survive bullies, racists and homophobes, and touch the world with a little moment of wearing heels on TV, imagine what more they could do to change the world. These were wonderful youngsters who were already dedicated to serving their communities. Their selfless volunteering and contribution to various causes is exactly the kind of citizenry the world needs.

I was inspired by their acts of goodwill and kindness at such a young age. At the end of my speech, as everyone clapped, I went into a random involuntary bow in front of the prince. I guess there was no escaping the inevitable Buckingham Palace faux pas. I'll never know where it came from; it certainly wasn't part of the brief.

Mum watched in awe as her little Johannes was applauded. The minute I stepped off stage, cameras were clamouring to take our picture. Most of the photographers wanted to capture me with Mum. Realising that she was a bit overwhelmed, I whispered words of reassurance.

'It's okay, Mum. No one is going to chew you up. They just want pictures,' I said.

I held her hand firmly and stayed glued to her side for the rest of the day. We then made our way to the catering area for some tea and cake. To Mum's horror, the tea was served in disposable plastic cups. Covid-19 had even changed the hospitality at Buckingham Palace, and Mum couldn't hide her surprise. I had to remind her that she was still wrapped in the Queen's blanket – something that returned a smile to her face.

The blanket story is one that will be told and retold for generations to come in the Radebe household. It is probably why, when we got home, the first thing Mum did after a long day of quietly processing all the attention was to relive the day. She boasted to Jabulile about the blanket, as well as how everyone in that room wanted to speak to us. I guess it's true that no matter what you achieve in this world, to your family, you will always remain one of theirs. And I wouldn't have it any other way.

After that outing, Mum resolved that she didn't need to go anywhere else. She had suffered the freezing conditions and seen the best part of England, taking tea in the manicured gardens of Buckingham Palace. As far as she was concerned, nothing could match that. Instead, Mum found things to do in my apartment. Jabulile and I would head out for lunches or sightseeing, and we would come back and my rug would be hanging from the balcony after a thorough scrub or the couches would have been washed. One day, Mum moved all the furniture and spring-cleaned the entire house. I tried to convince her to take the time off and relax, but cleaning is one of the things Mum enjoys above all. During her two-week stay, Mum washed my clothes, and even folded my socks and underwear. When I protested that I was an adult and didn't require this level of fuss, she said I was her son and there is nothing she doesn't know about me. Once a mummy's boy, always a mummy's boy.

Although I would have loved to see Mum rest for a change, I must admit it was nice to be doted on and to see her make her mark on my new home. When she was not busy with chores, she would watch her favourite new British show, *The Repair Shop*, for hours as they repaired cherished possessions.

The next time Mum stepped outside was for our *Hello!* magazine photo shoot. We had agreed to the feature long before

Mum even left for the UK. She understood as much as I did that this was one commitment neither one of us could go back on. *Hello!* magazine had been such an integral part of sharing my story with the world and I am grateful to journalists like Sally Morgan, who took a shine to me from my first year on *Strictly*. Two years earlier, the magazine had even visited me and Mum in Zamdela for my first magazine feature with her.

For the latest shoot, they had organised an entire glam squad for all three of us. We shot in various landmarks around London, which was a brilliant way to show Mum the city. We went to St Paul's Cathedral and Mum screamed with joy, flagging that it was the church in which Princess Diana got married. We then went to the River Thames, Trafalgar Square and the London Eye. It was the only way Mum would have seen the city, and I was happy that it had worked out.

On the day of the shoot, we christened Mum's wig 'Naomi Campbell' and Jabulile's 'Oprah Winfrey'. It was mind-blowing to see how transformed they were after being styled by the exceptional team at *Hello!* The shoot went swell, and the magazine staff even offered my mum and sister the Naomi and Oprah to take home.

A few days before Mum and Jabu left for South Africa, I was asked to do my first *Hello!* Pride cover. It was the first time the title had released a digital Pride special edition, and I was to be the first cover star. The team was brilliantly consultative, checking with me on the visuals to accompany my story – something of a novel experience. They wanted me to be part of the styling of the images, which empowered me to want to do something bold and distinct from my other shoots. No longer did I want to look like the boy next door. Instead, I wanted to capture what was going on in my head, so I told them I wanted to wear a dress for one of my looks and sent them references of how I wanted my hair and nails done, which I said I would take care of. I took Jabu with me for some pampering while I got my hair and nails done. I got back with my hair adorned with extensions and my nails polished. I was prepared to face my mum's silent judgement. Mounting a pre-emptive defence of my look, I walked in and immediately declared that what my hair looked like was not the final picture, as it was still going to be styled properly the next day. She seemed remarkably nonplussed and carried on with her seemingly endless housework.

In the studio, I was ecstatic to see it all come together just as I had imagined. The hair, the nails and the red feathery chiffon dress with stilettos brought me immense joy. Since the days of dressing my Barbies, fashion has long been an obsession. At the studio, we played Beyoncé, Rihanna and some other favourite divas to further lift the spirited energy in the studio. Outside of the *Priscilla, Queen of the Desert* dance piece on *Strictly*, it was the boldest I had been in expressing myself. I felt gorgeous. I stood proudly, my six-foot-four figure in a red dress and heels. For once, I didn't feel like hiding any part of it. Not the dress, not the heels, make-up or nails. I have never felt more myself.

At the end of the shoot, I returned the outfits to the stylist and decided not to remove my make-up or touch my hair. I was going to step out into the world in the fullness and finery of how I felt inside.

Heading back home that day, it dawned on me that my mum had never really experienced any of my life-changing moments as they had happened. Being a world away in South Africa meant that everything was refracted through the TV screen. She had not once been in the studio in the UK or on our tours to see it happen live. This would be one of the first times she would see me in my new natural environment, in my element.

I was nervous, but not enough to change anything about how I looked that day. I walked into the house and this time I didn't want to justify or soften the moment. It was my sister Jabulile who latched on to it before my mum or I could.

'Must you look this hot? No, this is sickening!' she said lovingly.

'Thank you,' I laughed.

My mum then asked how my day had been and how the shoot went. I said it went well and headed to my room. This is how I know that my mum is one of the most special people in my life and so deeply connected to me. She is one of the few people with a genuine interest in my well-being, knows brilliantly how to read me and senses when I am not okay. In no time at all, she followed me to my room and sat on my bed. She told me that she wanted to really know how my day had gone. She had the look I had seen over the years, the one that said 'tell me everything'.

'First and foremost, you must not judge me,' I said, still lying on the bed.

'Since when am I the judge?' she said with furrowed eyebrows.

I gave her a look.

'Mum, today I felt really good about myself. I had such an amazing time on that set getting dressed up and made up,' I said.

I then reached for my phone and showed Mum pictures of myself in the red dress, with gold heels, and the live reel of me playing with red lace. There was one full picture of me standing tall in that red outfit where we both stopped and gasped.

'You look beautiful, Baba,' she said with such conviction that I carried on talking about the shoot. My mouth continued to babble, but my mind clung to her words.

I had waited my entire life to hear my mum say those words. Over the years, she had told me she loved me, that I was enough and lots of other important things little boys who wear heels and play with Barbie dolls need to hear. But this was the first time Mum was telling me I looked beautiful in cross-dressing.

Without missing a beat, Mum asked me to send her the picture, to which I asked what she wanted to do with it.

'I want to show your uncle. We have shared with him pictures of everything we have done so far. I think it's only fair that we show him this beautiful moment as well,' she said.

I let out a huge sigh of relief and laughed at how casually Mum had requested that picture. There was no antagonism or ill will. I was left with a feeling of something more than acceptance – she had embraced me. I was her son, and she loved me without shame. No apologies and no explanation required. And that was that.

I didn't want to wash off my make-up that day. I slept with a full face and covered myself with a blanket of my family's love. I was one of the fortunate ones. I felt happier than I could express. My heart broke for all of those who were not going to bed that night with that blanket of love and acceptance. Change is possible and the world is full of wonderful surprises.

The next day, Mum and Jabulile packed their bags, and we squeezed into a black cab and made our way to the airport. Their trip, and the months leading up to it, had been a dream come true. For as long as I've worked abroad, I had always yearned for my family to share in my life experiences. What good were my adventures if I couldn't share them with my loved ones? I cried tears of joy. I cried because it had all been so perfect. Mum and Jabulile were concerned about my emotional turn, so Jabulile offered to stay if I wanted her to. I told them to press on.

I would be fine.

Chapter Fourteen

Finally Home

When I sat down with the producers and saw the success of *Freedom* on paper in black and white, my dream was realised. My first thought was, 'I can buy my mum a house.'

My producers treated me so fairly, and I felt incredibly proud of what we had achieved. We had told the joyous stories of our culture and ritual celebrations and the song and dance that permeate every stage of our lives at home. Another headline show was on the cards. I was still shocked by the response to the show from audiences and critics alike, and delighted by the fact that I would be allowed more creative freedom with a larger budget to fill bigger venues, along with more ornate and opulent costumes and louder sounds. I knew that the new show needed to be like the original because the message resonated with the audiences who had been to see it. There would be time to do a different production in the future. This would be the show that I would have put on originally if I'd had the money to do so.

'Let's unleash it,' I said, and thus, the name of the new tour, *Freedom Unleashed*, was born. We would be turning the glitter dial right up!

It was important that we announced it as soon as possible after the original tour to ride on the waves of success we had seen, so the wheels were set in motion. I went on *The Graham Norton Show* and sat on the sofa with Salma Hayek, Shania Twain and Julianne Moore to promote the new show. It was thanks to Graham that *Freedom* tickets had sold so well, so it felt important to thank him. He has such an incredible reach. I find the whole experience of sitting on sofas with A-listers just wild. It is by far the scariest show I do.

During that year's awards season, John and I were invited to the British LGBT Awards, where we were honourees. The lovely Shirley Ballas presented the Media Moment of the Year award to me and John – a thrilling surprise for us.

Shortly after that, we went on to win the Game Changer award at the Attitude Awards, after which the Ethnicity Awards recognised me as an Inspirational Public Figure. When I read the list of nominees, I couldn't get over it; the other people on that list are icons in my eyes. Delighted, I called Mum and told her that we were on a winning streak.

Strictly rehearsals kicked back off in July 2022. I've had so many beautiful journeys over the years with my partners, but after my experience with John, it left me wondering whether I would ever experience the kind of ride that I had had with him with anyone else. Nonetheless, I still approached the series with the same excitement I feel each year and was very happy to be partnered with the comedian and writer Ellie Taylor. Ellie came with no dance training.

'What *am* I doing?' she regularly lamented during the early rehearsals, as I think it slowly dawned on her that she would soon be dancing in front of an audience of millions.

'Girl, you signed up for this,' I would laugh.

'But Johannes, this dancing lark is hard.'

She is right, of course, it is hard, and sometimes it can look far easier from the comfort of the sofa at home than it is. What really helped me was the realisation that Ellie would throw herself into it. As a teacher, I can tell quickly whether this will be the case, and Ellie worked hard. Her heart was right there for every second of each day.

'The quicker you get used to those shoes, the better,' I told her in the first week.

I knew on the first Saturday show, when she did not take off her shoes once, that she had the commitment and determination to go the distance.

We had fun with it. For the first time on *Strictly*, there was laughter that bubbled up from deep inside me and spilled out throughout our rehearsal times. It had taken until that series for me to feel like I no longer needed to prove myself. Ellie also made me feel so at ease.

'It's so lovely being paired up with you,' she would tell me regularly. Ellie came for the experience, which then allowed me to do the job I loved and be on my A-game. Even now, after all my years of competing, I feel it is an honour every time I hit the stage.

As we progressed through the series, I wanted to know if we could make it to the glitterball. During the show in Blackpool in week nine, there was a mishap with our American Smooth routine.

'I would really like to go home today,' Ellie said as we left the stage.

'What?'

'I just don't think I am as good as everybody else,' she replied.

'You stop right there,' I ordered. 'You have given everything to this competition and journey. You deserve to be here just as much as everyone else.'

I was ready to fight for our partnership and place on the show harder than ever. The following week, because of the strength of the competition, if we landed in the bottom two, we knew we would be going out. We could only hope for the best, so when we were up against Fleur East and Vito Coppola, it was our time. Being sent home before the end never gets easier. It's just terrible. The sense of FOMO is enormous, and sometimes I wonder whether people recover. I always have in my head who should win. Like the rest of the world, you start supporting those who you feel deserve the glitterball trophy. Sometimes we pick the people who go on to win, but often we don't. The public is in charge, after all, and I know the votes are not only about the technical precision of the dancing involved.

During the *Strictly* rehearsals period, I was asked to take part in a celebrity Christmas spin-off of the BBC show *The Great British Sewing Bee*. It is one of my favourite shows that makes me feel warm and cosy inside. Whatever is going on outside, when I watch it, the world is just fine. I was so excited when I was asked;

I wanted to do it and win. As soon as the call came, I bought myself a new sewing machine to practise with. The soft and continuous whirring sound reminded me of my Aunt Ruth, one of my mum's sisters. She was a dressmaker who worked in a Johannesburg boutique. We spent the least time of all with this auntie because she would get up at the crack of dawn to go to work and then come home late at night, only to get straight back on to that sewing machine. Sometimes she would come to our home, and I would fall asleep with the low and rhythmic clicking sound as the needle penetrated the fabric. She made everything in that shop, from lavish gowns to stunning scarves and skirts. She was so talented but never made clothes for herself. I practised through the nights to make my lines straighter. I find the process so therapeutic. I could lose myself for a whole day. It reminded me of the joy I found making my little Barbie clothes as a child. It is so satisfying to create something unique that looks good.

I jumped on the train from London with my sewing machine and joined Natalie Cassidy, Penny Lancaster, Rosie Ramsey and the judges in the studio in Leeds. Everything I felt watching the show was real when I was there. It was only September, but it was chilly outside, and the studio exuded warmth and fun. It already felt like Christmas.

We were tasked with making three items: an apron for the pattern challenge, in which I made a tartan number for my mum; a Christmas-themed baby outfit; and New Year's Eve costumes inspired by our favourite pop stars. I love Harry Styles because he is liberated. He wears what he likes and doesn't care what people think. I was celebrating that about him and made a sparkling, open-necked one-piece. When the judge, Esme Young, asked if I sewed at home, I was so flattered. I was delighted to be crowned the winner, and it sparked something inside me – I haven't stopped sewing since. Now I alter costumes and make shirts. I hope to make time in the future to hone this skill further.

Another career pinnacle was when I was invited to a State Banquet at Buckingham Palace during the state visit for the President of South Africa. It read: 'The Lord Chamberlain has received His Majesty's command to invite Mr Johannes Radebe to a State Banquet to be given at Buckingham Palace by the King and the Queen Consort in honour of the President of the Republic of South Africa and Dr Tshepo Motsepe on Tuesday, 22nd November 2022, at 8.30pm.'

I know – I mean, when the invitation arrived, I called my agent Ant immediately.

'I've been invited to a State Banquet at Buckingham Palace!' I said, shocked at this beautiful, embossed invite in my hand.

'I don't believe you. Send me a picture,' he said, laughing.

It was true. It was from the King to me. We were flabbergasted. It was a lot of diplomats and politicians and me. The list read: diplomat, diplomat, diplomat, diplomat's spouse . . . dancer. I almost died.

If there was any time that my mum would say, 'Take a bow and pat yourself on the back,' it would be this moment.

First, came the decision of what to wear and, when I read the word 'banquet', I wondered whether I could go in a ball gown or full African regalia, complete with a headdress. But it was a strict white-tie dress code, so I went to hire myself one. I went full-out. As soon as I walked into the shop, the man looked me up and down, and pulled out the perfect suit. It fitted like a glove and made me feel like a million dollars.

I don't know why they chose me to go, but what I do know was the incredible welcome I received when I returned to Buckingham Palace.

'It is lovely to see you again,' the staff told me.

'This is mad,' I thought to myself silently. The first time I had been to the palace, I had my mum and Ant with me, but this time, I was all alone. I would only be allowed a spouse. So single Jojo it was.

'The King will see you later,' a member of staff told me.

As soon as I walked through the room, everyone flocked to me. They all wanted to talk to me about *Strictly* and how the season was going. Many of the diplomats apologised for the fact that they were not up to date because, as the world opened up, they had been busy travelling. Everyone wanted to talk about the previous year when, due to Covid restrictions, it felt like the whole world had tuned in to see series nineteen of the show. I stood there for what felt like an eternity with all these voices coming at me, asking me about John and 2021.

There was one point when I looked up, and the room sparkled. There, in the distance, was the Princess of Wales, and the light glinted off her headpiece. She was a real-life angel and carried herself with such poise and grace. I was captivated. Almost the whole Royal Family was there: King Charles and the Queen

Consort, the Prince and Princess of Wales and the Earl and Countess of Wessex (now the Duke and Duchess of Edinburgh).

When we were seated at the table, we stood and sang both the British and South African national anthems. Then the King stood and spoke, welcoming everyone in all the South African languages.

He said: 'Avuxeni, dumela, sawubona, molo, molweni, ndaa. My wife and I are delighted to welcome you to Buckingham Palace this evening.'

When he said 'dumela' – *hello* in my language – I almost did a loud squeal and had to remind myself where I was.

I thought to myself, 'Charles, even if I didn't know you, you got me now.'

He gave the most wonderful speech, which talked about our late Queen, who had not long passed, and her visit to Cape Town on her twenty-first birthday, where she pledged her life to the service of the people of the Commonwealth. It was the first State Banquet that he and the Queen Consort had hosted, and that felt quite poignant. He spoke of the late Queen's admiration for South Africa's vibrancy, diversity and natural beauty, and went on to talk about the links between the two countries.

He brought up the legacy of the great South African, former Archbishop Desmond Tutu, and his saying: 'My humanity is bound up in yours, for we can only be human together.' By that point of the speech, I was practically in tears on the floor.

I had a lovely time eating the delicious food and chatting with the spouses I was sitting next to. They kept trying to tell me that we needed to find the ballroom to do some dancing.

After dinner, we were then invited to see the King. One of the staff took my mobile phone. I should have asked what the protocol was, as no one else seemed to have a phone, but then again, I'm not a diplomat, so I'm not sure how I would ever know. It would be typical that my mum would call mid-conversation with the King, asking if I had met him yet.

I couldn't see what other people were doing when they met him, so when I went round the corner, I greeted him with a full bum-almost-to-the-floor curtsy. It was like a full ballroom presentation. It was the way he picked me up with his eyes as I hovered near the ground, with a soft smile on his face.

'Good evening, Your Majesty, how are you?' I asked, trying to hold it together.

'Johannes, welcome back to Buckingham Palace,' he said.

I couldn't understand how he knew my name or the fact I had been to Buckingham Palace before. I felt like I was having an out-of-body experience.

'Really welcome. My wife would really like to talk to you,' he added.

Between the King and the Queen Consort stood my president, President Ramaphosa, who was smiling, but I could tell in his eyes that he was thinking, 'Who are you?'

'Ke thabela ho o bona,' I said. *I am happy to see you.*

He replied that he was happy to see me too. And all I could hear was my mum's voice in my ear saying, 'Tell him we still have no electricity, Baba. We are load-shedding.'

Then I moved along the line to the Queen Consort.

'How could you be here?' she smiled. 'Johannes, why are you

not rehearsing?' She was worried that the banquet was cutting into my practice time.

'I wouldn't miss this for the world,' I told her.

We continued talking.

'I used all my three votes on you during the Blackpool week,' she told me. 'I didn't want you and Ellie to leave.'

That set my night.

I went off to mingle in the room, unsure of who to talk to, but soon found myself in small groups, finding common ground. the Earl of Wessex also approached with a spring in his step, saying he needed to get his wife, too. Sophie bounded over, took my hand and jumped straight into more *Strictly* chat. She told me that she had also voted for us during Blackpool week. The idea of the palace phones being rung off the hook for me and Ellie made my heart soar.

Someone once told me about the Proverbs passage in the Bible that reads, 'A man's gift makes room for him and brings him before the great.' Never had that phrase been truer. I was completely humbled and blown away by how far my dance had taken me.

The day after the *Strictly* finals, where Hamza Yassin and Jowita Przystal lifted the glitterball, I flew home for Christmas.

It was the second year since my Aunt Martha had passed and we tried to uphold the traditions that she had put into place. The day was not the same, though. There was not the sort of order in place, and that was disappointing. I also struggle now as life has changed for me beyond recognition from my days in South Africa. I have tried to encourage family members to give me their CVs, so I can help them find different jobs away from the townships through my contacts on cruise ships and in other places, but they have not been forthcoming. I have always wanted to help and do more, but the problem of where it stops weighs heavily and is something I still grapple with. It's a huge adjustment for me to move between my two worlds.

The day I returned home was the day my mum moved into her new home. She didn't want to move to a new location, so the inside of our old house where I grew up was completely remodelled and extended. Over the years, I slowly built a two-bedroom annexe and bathroom space in the yard for when I came home so that I could have a bit more space or other people could use it when I was not there. My sister, mum, niece and nephew moved into it for two months while the work was being done. I was quite happy to avoid the cement and the dust, thank you very much. Outside, Mummy has her stone pillars, like her own version of Buckingham Palace, and she is delighted with that. It is so grand when you look at the transformation. There is no doubt from anyone in our town that this is Jocobeth Ramagole's residence.

A couple of days before Christmas, a dining room set with a long table and eight chairs arrived. Before, if it rained, we would all cram inside to try to find space to sit or stand. Now we could sit around the table together and, on Christmas Day, when we finally sat down to eat, there was room for many people.

*   *   *

Creating *Freedom Unleashed* was incredible. I drafted in a brilliant team of creatives but, of course, nothing ever runs smoothly. The budget was blown out of the water for the costumes, but there were still some things I wanted to change. I'm not sure if it would have turned out quite so well if I had not pushed so hard. I took out my sewing machine and called on every contact I know who creates beautiful things and, in two weeks, we turned the costumes around. I was still taking in trousers an hour before the curtain went up for the opening show in Southampton. My mind was also blown when the producer's opening night gift to me was a giant touring truck – it had a giant poster with my face on it.

I loved the certainty that people were going to come to the show. There were none of the unknowns of the first show. I no longer had to start from the beginning. The people were coming and they knew what it was about, and I adored the fact I could spend time in the show focusing on the joy and energy of all types of African music and dance, like pantsula and kizomba. It felt like one big party. I had an incredible cast around me, including the singer Duane-Lamonte O'Garro and the South African singer and songwriter Ramelo, who came over to the UK, leaving her small child at home to be on tour. The idea that people could come to watch the show and feel accepted for whatever their differences may be made me deeply appreciative. They radiated that acceptance back at me. What a joy that was for me.

Being back on the road with the show was amazing. Seeing people come back felt so special. There is one lady who saw the show fifteen times. As every artist will say, I try to reflect the times and wanted the show to resonate with people. In that show, it was like I had found my people. And we were sold out every night.

All cities are surprising. In York, the theatre was small, but the energy was so mighty. It felt like a crowd ten times as big. Stoke was one of the loudest cheers I have ever had. The noise always surprises me, and I think, 'What have I done?' And at that stage, I had not done anything except walk onto the stage! On our final show night in Dublin, the audience would not let me leave the stage and sung back to me. It was truly incredible.

I have also realised that people are on this journey with me. I don't think anyone in my audience will understand that they make me feel seen. The idea that a dancer can headline a show still seems unfathomable to me.

In 2024, I will create a new show, *The House of Jojo*, that will make space for everyone of all ages, sizes and ethnicities. I know people have been stopped from pursuing their dreams for these reasons. Now that I have a home in the industry, I want to welcome people into my home. I also plan to take *Freedom Unleashed* to Johannesburg and a couple of the townships. I know that not everyone can travel that far, so by going to the townships with a downscaled production, I will be able to reach more people. It also means that I can finally shake my tush in front of all my friends and family at home.

I want to look out into the audience and into the eyes of the children so they understand and feel that their dreams are valid. Self-expression should have no fear. I want to show them that they do not need to stay in any lane; they can break out and be themselves – whatever that looks or feels like to them. They can walk this life not thinking it is too big and that their aspirations are unobtainable. Most of all, I want to say to them: Darling, how will you ever know what you can do if you do not try? There is no limit to what you can achieve.

Acknowledgements

First and foremost, to my family – thank you for your unconditional love.

To my Aunt Martha – for taking us in when we had nowhere to go.

To my dance parents, Patricia and Elvis Paleman – thank you for nurturing a generation of dancers.

To my *Burn the Floor* family, Nic Notley and Peta Roby – thank you for launching my dance career internationally. I will be forever indebted to you.

To Modiehi, Magauta, Thami, Barbara, Megan and Jeanne – your passion for dance inspires me. What an honour to have danced with all of you.

Thanks to my community of Zamdela – 'It takes a village to raise a Fabulous Child'.

To Londekile Ntsiba – I wouldn't have finished my high school if you weren't there, thank you.

To Tebogo Kgobokoe – thank you for teaching us about Black excellence.

To my dear friends, Jeff, Seun and Carl – thank you for the gift of friendship.

To Jane Fry and Nicolette Bosch – thank you for the support and for believing in me.

To Kee-Leen Irvine and the Rapid Blue family – thank you for the introduction and guidance in the television industry.

To my *Strictly* family and our Executive Producer Sarah James – thank you for inviting me into your sparkling and magical world of joy and opportunity.

LeAnne Dlamini, Leigh-Anne Williams, Vanes-Mari du Toit, Catherine Tyldesley, Caroline Quinton, John Whaite and Ellie Taylor – thank you for my *Strictly* adventures.

To Ant, my amazing agent, there every step of the way, and everyone at Olivia Bell Management – thank you for making all of this possible.

To Royo, my tour producers – thank you for giving me my *Freedom*.

To Amanda Malpass and Alex Buchanan PR – thank you for the incredible media opportunities.

To Lauren, Emma, Alice, Christian, Naomi, Will, Claudette, and everyone at Hodder – thank you for giving me this chance to tell my story and I hope, inspire others.

To Paul – thank you for your time and for joining me on this writing journey. To George – thank you for the beautiful editorial input.

And finally, to everyone who has supported me – thank you for all your love along the way. Without you, I would not be where I am today. I am eternally grateful to have you by my side on this wild adventure.

Love,

Jojo x

Picture Acknowledgements

Pages 1–8: All courtesy of the Author

Page 9: (*top*) © BBC Photo Library; (*bottom*) © BBC Photo Library

Page 10: © Mike Marsland / WireImage / Getty Images

Page 11: (*top*) © Jonathan Brady – WPA Pool / Getty Images; (*bottom*) © The Duke of Edinburgh's Award / Rachel Palmer

Page 12: (*top*) © BBC Photo Library; (*bottom*) © PA Images / Alamy Stock Photo

Page 13: © Louise Morris / Alamy Stock Photo

Page 14: © Ken McKay / ITV / Shutterstock

Page 15: (*top*) © Liz McAulay, Camera Press London; (*bottom*) © Liz McAulay, Camera Press London

Page 16: © Elliott Wilcox